A Sky Full of
Starlings

A Sky Full of Starlings

A Diary of the Birding Year

STEPHEN MOSS

First published 2008 by
Aurum Press Ltd, 7 Greenland Street, London NW1 0ND
www.aurumpress.co.uk

Relief prints as chapter openers by Carry Akroyd

A catalogue record for this book is available
from the British Library.

ISBN 978 1 84513 353 5

1 3 5 7 9 10 8 6 4 2
2008 2010 2012 2011 2009

Designed and typeset in Fournier by M Rules

Printed and bound in Great Britain by
MPG Books, Bodmin

In memory of Christopher Helm: a fine birder, great publisher and true gentleman.

And for Nigel and Cheryle Redman: his dear friends, and mine.

Contents

Prologue

31 DECEMBER 2007

Mill Batch, Mark, Somerset

In a few minutes, I shall be Buzz Lightyear.

It's almost dusk, on New Year's Eve. In a little while, against my better judgement, I shall be putting on the costume of the celebrated superhero in preparation for a fancy dress party we're hosting tonight for some close friends. But with an hour or so before the guests arrive, I have managed to escape from the noise and bustle of the house, and come into the garden for a few moments' break.

There is the usual activity I would expect on any late afternoon in the middle of winter. The Rooks are cawing high in the ash trees, a Blackbird is chattering loudly from the brambles, and a little group of Long-tailed Tits are working their way along the pollarded willows bordering the eastern edge of the garden, twittering as they go. Earlier today I heard a Song Thrush singing – the first sign of spring, and another indication that this mild winter weather is having a topsy-turvy effect on the lifecycles of our common birds.

I sit quietly on the garden bench I inherited from my mother, looking and listening. This is where I usually come when I need a spot of rest and recreation, and from where I have seen – and heard – many of the birds that visit our garden, or fly through its airspace.

Then, as dusk falls, I wander back to the house – and to the light, sound and joy of a family New Year. A flock of Starlings passes overhead like a wartime RAF squadron returning from a raid, each bird silhouetted against the sky. And just before I shut the door on the old year, a Robin sings to me from the hedge by the lane. It's my last bird of 2007 – a fine year for birds and birding.

This episode marks the end of a year during which I kept a diary of my birding experiences: some here in my garden; others elsewhere in my home county of Somerset; and a few beyond. I have done this partly for my own pleasure; but also, I hope, for yours.

For although it is true that birding can be a solitary, private activity, it is also made up of shared, communal experiences. Sometimes this sharing is literal, as when we go birding with an old friend. But more often than not it is because every encounter with birds – whether an everyday or once-in-a-lifetime experience – adds to our collective memory. By chronicling these events over the course of a single calendar year, and revealing my own thoughts and feelings, I hope that some of these will resonate with your own.

In recent years I have come to realise that birding is not something you 'go out and do', but something you *are*. My friend and fellow birder Sean Dooley summed it up perfectly in his book *The Big Twitch* when he wrote:

When people find out I am a birdwatcher, they often ask me where I go birdwatching, as if it is something that happens elsewhere, beyond the realm of everyday life.

Whereas, as any birder knows, birds are always with you. You begin birding when you awake, and stop when you fall asleep – and even then, some of us dream about birds!

So I hope you enjoy what follows: a diary of one birder's year, during which I travelled to the high tops of the Cairngorms, back to my old haunts in the London suburbs, and to my favourite place of all, North Norfolk. Amongst these excursions I also reveal how, day-by-day, I discovered the joys and delights of the area around my new home, in the heart of the Somerset Levels.

There are many wonderful experiences here, yet my favourite birding moments are those that arose out of a completely unrelated event: mowing the lawn, taking the children to the local park, or going to the pictures in Weston-super-Mare. For it is by these arbitrary, unpredictable encounters with birds that our lives are, I believe, continually enhanced.

January

Somerset Moors and Levels

B irders sometimes find themselves in funny places – and in rather unusual company. So it was that at half past ten in the morning on New Year's Day, I sat in the Bay View Café in Burnham-on-Sea – a sporadically charming seaside resort a few miles west of my home. I was enjoying a coffee and eating a bacon sandwich, in the presence of two waitresses and a dog. Oh, and fifty members of the local cycling club.

Despite our sartorial differences – I was wearing the standard birding gear of fleece, jacket, boots and binoculars; they were clad in the colourful uniforms that denote the serious cyclist – we had more in common than the casual observer might assume.

For who else, apart from obsessive enthusiasts, crawls out of bed before first light on New Year's Day? Who else ignores the throbbing pain in their temples, caused by over-indulgence the night before? And who else looks forward to this day as a chance to start again, to begin a clean slate, and kick off the year as they mean to go on?

By the time we converged on the Burnham café for a welcome spot of sustenance, the cyclists and I had already enjoyed an eventful morning. They had done a quick circuit of north-west Somerset, giving thanks to the lull in the wet and windy weather that made December a washout. I, too, had done a circuit – though using four wheels rather than two – and by the time I ticked off Feral Pigeon along the seafront, had already racked up 50 different species of bird in just over two hours. Numbers, of course, are not everything. But it is a tradition – going back over a century now – that on New Year's Day we birders tally up how many species we can see.

This 1 January, my sense of anticipation was even greater; for this was the very first New Year at our new home on the Somerset Levels. We came here last July, partly to be nearer to my job at the BBC Natural History Unit in Bristol; partly to give our three young children more room than a crowded semi in the London suburbs; and partly, I must admit, to be somewhere with plenty of birds.

Our new home is the sort of place I have always dreamed of living in: an eighteenth century farmhouse, complete with hot and cold running mice. It also has a garden – more accurately a series of gardens – that extends over more than an acre. What was once a neatly trimmed lawn, mown to within an inch of its life by the previous owners, is now half rough grass and half hay meadow. I prefer it that way – not only is it less work, but it's also much better for wildlife. At least that's my excuse.

As I write, the house is in its usual state of chaos – due mainly to the presence of three small children who can reduce a neat, tidy room to something resembling a bomb-site in just a few minutes. Outside, three year old Charlie's tractor is strategically placed behind my car; while in the back garden George and Daisy, now almost two, have deposited a range of plastic toys, dolls and other playthings across the lawn.

Charlie, George and Daisy will, I am sure, play their part in this year's birding chronicles, as of course will my wife Suzanne, who still manages to notice birds from time to time, despite her almost constant childcare duties.

Our house is situated on the east side of Mark, allegedly the longest village in England, though other villages have been known to make the same claim. We are on the northern edge of the Somerset Levels, the portion known, at least to the local tourist board, as the Avalon Marshes. This is where the mythical King Arthur is supposed to be buried, and where the historical figure of King Alfred famously burnt the cakes. We are roughly equidistant from Cheddar, Glastonbury, Wells and Burnham-on-Sea, and about 20 minutes drive, or about three quarters of an hour's cycle, from each.

To the north, we are bordered by the Mendips, one of the highest of which, Crook's Peak, we can see from the back garden (and which is already known to the family as 'Charlie's Mountain'). To the south, slightly farther away, lie the Polden Hills – a shallow ridge of high ground separating the Avalon Marshes from Sedgemoor. It's a great location for birds, as I am just starting to discover – and fortunately one of the very best places of all is my own garden.

So, just as it has been for the past few decades, it was with a sense of child-like anticipation that I opened the back door, moments after dawn, and gazed up into the sky to see which bird would herald the New Year.

The first bird I saw – and indeed heard, 'chacking' in the early morning air – was a Jackdaw. I have always had a soft spot for Jackdaws, ever since I encountered a tame one as a toddler, so it seemed like a good sign. The next bird, coming seconds afterwards, was a Magpie, a flash of black-and-white as it swooped across the lawn.

Hard on its heels was one of the classic birds of this part of Somerset, and indeed emblematic of the whole of the English countryside. Even in semi-darkness I could pick out the blue-black plumage, raggedy wings and pale face-patch of a third member of the crow family: the Rook.

By the time I left home, half an hour later, I had added another dozen or so species, including a Green Woodpecker whose laughing call drowned out the distant cock crowing. I would have liked to stay longer, but the rapidly lightening sky drew me away and out onto the Somerset Levels, the truly wild landscape just a short distance – as the Rook flies – from my home.

Tealham Moor is already one of my favourite spots. It lies just south of a ridge of high ground known as the Isle of Wedmore: a classic stretch of flat, low-lying land that floods in winter, it is now managed mainly for wildlife.

Back in September I enjoyed a cycle ride along one of the many broad, straight 'droves' – ancient rights of way that criss-cross the moors – with Yellow Wagtails, Whinchats and Clouded Yellow butterflies for company. But by January these summer visitors were long gone, and the drove I had cycled down was under a couple of feet of water. The flooded fields, to either side of the rough road, played host to a fine selection of classic winter birds.

There were Lapwings, whose vast flocks contained a few Golden Plover – their smaller size and long, tapering wings making them easy to pick out, even at a distance; our two wintering thrushes, Redwings and Fieldfares, the latter uttering a loud, harsh chatter from time to time; and the odd Buzzard, foraging for food in the muddy fields.

As I watched the first sunrise of the new year light up the watery landscape, and Glastonbury Tor emerge in the distance to the south-east, it occurred to me that this scene has hardly changed for hundreds of years; at least since the land around me was reclaimed from the sea back in the Middle Ages.

It's a thought I have frequently – at least a lot more frequently than I ever had on my old stamping-ground in south-west London. Here in Somerset I feel, in some vague, still rather unformed sense, part of the landscape. It's a feeling that enhances my birding experience, as I hope to reveal over the coming year.

My reverie was broken by a harsh, deep, throaty sound – the unmistakable call of the largest member of the crow tribe. Looking up, I could see a huge black silhouette, with distinctive broad wings, huge head and wedge-shaped tail. It was a Raven, a good bird this far away from the Mendips, its usual home.

Later that morning, just before returning home, I finally caught up with a rare visitor to the region: the long-staying Great Northern Diver at Cheddar Reservoir. I had heard about this via the website of the Somerset Ornithological Society – known inevitably as the SOS. The website contains a Messageboard on which local birders regularly post their sightings: ranging from a scarce bird in their garden, through the arrivals and departures of summer and winter visitors, to news of some major rarity. Since I moved here the SOS website has helped me see most of the unusual temporary residents, including this wintering Great Northern Diver.

Even so, I had to scan for a while before I finally saw the giant waterbird. Rather like a large, pale Cormorant, it appeared somewhat incongruous as it swam along on this inland water, at a time when most of its kind were wintering off our coasts.

So overall, despite the limited time I had available on this first day of the year, I enjoyed some memorable moments. There was the first Skylark I have heard since moving here last summer, a large flock of dabbling ducks at Catcott Lows, and best of all, a Little Egret over the garden when I returned home – floating high overhead on its Persil-white wings, legs trailing behind it. Little Egrets may now be as common as herons, but I still feel that spark of involuntary surprise every time I see this Mediterranean bird on my local patch.

Catcott Lows, Somerset

It had rained all morning and the forecast for Sunday was even worse. So when the skies began to lighten a couple of hours before dusk I was itching to get out, even if only for a short time.

Finally, at three p.m., I grabbed my telescope and binoculars and headed south to Catcott Lows. As its name suggests, this area is even more low-lying than its surroundings, which makes it very wet indeed. In January the roads leading to it are half tarmac, half mud – and all water, reminding me why I never bother to clean my car.

Here, the Somerset Wildlife Trust has created a delightful little reserve, which in winter is mainly flooded, and whose shallow water is ideal for dabbling duck. On this visit the dominant species, as usual, was the Wigeon, with perhaps 1200 birds swimming on the water or grazing on the surrounding grassland, and filling the damp air with their whistling calls.

There were also plenty of Teal and Shoveler, and 50 or so Pintail, the males glowing orange-pink in the late afternoon light as they bobbed and displayed to the accompanying females.

Looking east from the hide, Glastonbury Tor stood out against the horizon in the milky sun, my telescope revealing tiny human figures around its base. Much nearer, at the back of the reserve, a flock of eight White-fronted Geese was feeding. Scarce birds in this area, whitefronts flee their Siberian breeding grounds each autumn, heading west to enjoy the benefits of our mild winter climate.

As I was watching the geese against the backdrop of the ancient tor, a fellow-birder pointed out a bird taking advantage of a more modern structure. Far away, to the left of the hide, a Peregrine was perched on top of a high pylon, surveying its hunting territory.

It did fly past us briefly, but, to our collective disappointment, decided not to stoop at the ducks. A large female Sparrowhawk was more cooperative, treating us to excellent views as it perched on a post and then flew right in front of the hide.

Earlier, I had seen an even more elusive raptor. As it shot through the air in front of a distant line of trees, its rapidly beating wings made me think it might be a wader. But as soon as I fixed my binoculars on the bird, its taut, compact shape and dark plumage made me realise it was our smallest falcon, the Merlin. It perched briefly on top of a tree, but before I could get a look through my telescope, it sped away.

The highlight of the day, as dusk fell, was the huge flocks of Lapwings. There were thousands of them in all, flying high overhead, before plunging down low over the water. With their contrasting plumage, dark green above and white below, they flashed alternately light and dark in the evening glow, before heading off to roost.

SATURDAY 13 JANUARY

Mill Batch, Mark, Somerset

As a birder, the joy of living somewhere new is that you never know quite what to expect. So far I haven't been disappointed: in just six months in our new home I've seen almost 60 species in, above or from the garden (the classic definition of a 'garden list'). To put this in per-spective, my total for five years in the west London suburb of Hampton was about 50.

There has been quality as well as quantity. All the classic garden birds are here, including several I had almost given up hope of seeing in my previous life, such as House Sparrow and Song Thrush.

The hedges to the west of our garden are home to a flock of about 50 sparrows, whose constant chirping is one of the most familiar yet delightful sounds made by any bird. And despite the ludicrously mild weather, our bird feeders have been full, with Chaffinches, Greenfinches and Goldfinches competing with the Great and Blue Tits for sunflower and nyger seeds.

Meanwhile the orchard next door is home to Green and Great Spotted Woodpeckers, while the mature ash trees at the end of the garden support a small rookery, and a family of Buzzards.

It's always worth looking up, too. As well as the Buzzards, flyover sightings have included a quartet of other raptors: Kestrel, Sparrowhawk, a single Hobby (back in July, a week or so after we moved in) and a couple of Peregrines, cruising past as if they own the place (obviously unaware that the property is in fact heavily mortgaged to the Cheltenham and Gloucester).

Then there are the gulls. You may share my wife Suzanne's point of view, that gulls are not really 'proper' birds, and are certainly not worth looking at in any detail. We shall have to agree to differ on this: for me, gulls are endlessly fascinating, and always worth a second glance.

So I was surprised when, standing in our front garden on a damp, grey Saturday morning, Suzanne drew my attention to a flock of about 50 gulls flying overhead. Surprised, and pleased – especially when I noticed, amongst the run-of-the-mill Black-headed and Common Gulls, a much scarcer species.

All-white wings, without a trace of black; a heavy, thick-set, dark bill; and that subtly different 'way of being' known to birders as 'jizz' – all pointed to an adult Mediterranean Gull.

Like the Little Egret I saw here the other day, Mediterranean Gull is a recent colonist to Britain. Once a real rarity, they first bred in the late 1960s; but unlike the egrets, are still fairly scarce. In a typical year in Somerset there might be a couple of dozen sightings, the vast majority on the coast.

So although I can forgive Suzanne for not sharing my enthusiasm at adding this bird to the garden list, I did allow myself a small, metaphorical punch of the air. Such modest triumphs and surprises are the stuff of birding. Context – the place, time and circumstances in which you see a bird – is everything.

Kennard Moor, Somerset

I had driven south, to a site just below Glastonbury Tor, to visit Beryl: not an elderly aunt, but a female Great Bustard. She isn't really called Beryl, though local birders frequently refer to her as such. Being originally from Russia, her official name is Galetchka, while she is also known as 'Orange 15', the number and colour of her plastic wingtag.

You may have guessed that Beryl/Galetchka isn't a truly wild bird, but one of the famous bustards of Salisbury Plain – part of a long-running attempt to return this magnificent species to our native avifauna. Apart from these birds, the nearest Great Bustards to our shores breed on the plains of central Spain, and in Eastern Europe. Until now, the only time I have ever seen the species was on a trip to Hungary more than a decade ago.

The reintroduction scheme has had its problems, with many of the early releases killed by foxes, but in the past couple of years more and more birds have reached adulthood. Outside the breeding season, they tend to wander, which explains Beryl's presence with a small flock of Mute Swans on the water meadows of Kennard Moor.

When I arrived, a carload of birders were already watching her as she grazed a few hundred yards away. Her orange wingtags (whose individual number allows her movements to be tracked) did slightly spoil the image; and as she was released here by human agency we can't officially count her on our lists.

Nevertheless, it was good to see her – and perhaps to glimpse a vision of the future, when free-flying flocks of British Great Bustards will fly past Stonehenge, and with luck, over my garden. I can but dream . . .

Edinburgh Airport

I'm on my way back from a work trip to Scotland when I hear some very sad news. Nigel Redman – a birder friend who is coming to stay with us this weekend – calls to let me know that our mutual friend Christopher Helm has been taken to hospital, and the prognosis doesn't look good.

By the time we awake the next morning, Nigel has had a call from Christopher's wife Amanda, with the news that he died in the night. We have a subdued breakfast, and reflect on the passing of a truly fine man.

Christopher had a long and distinguished career as a publisher of bird books. There can hardly be a birder in the country who does not own at least one of his volumes – under various imprints, including Croom Helm, Christopher Helm, Pica Press and finally, simply Helm. Glancing at random along my own bookshelves reveals that at least one third of my book collection comes from his stable. From specialist identification manuals to 'where to watch' guides, Christopher helped fuel the late 20th-century boom in natural history publishing and, as a consequence, in birding itself.

In person, he was equally extraordinary. Immensely tall, patrician, with the faintest trace of his native Scots accent overlaid by an education at my old college at Cambridge, Gonville and Caius, he was, quite simply, one of the most genuinely charming men I have ever known.

He could also be incredibly kind. A couple of decades ago, Nigel had to give up his job as a full-time birding tour leader to look after his infant daughter Emily. On discovering this, Christopher immediately offered him a job in his new publishing firm Pica Press. When Christopher eventually retired, Nigel moved to A&C Black, where the Helm imprint continues to this day.

Nigel reminds me that the two of them had long made a habit of going out on 1 January, for a day's birding around their homes in Kent and Sussex. Indeed they did so this New Year, including a visit to Dungeness to see Christopher's favourite bird, that exquisite black and white duck the Smew – on what turned out to be Christopher's last day's birding.

Christopher also knew a huge amount about birds. I remember sitting with him during the 'Bird Brain of Britain' contest at the Birdfair a few years ago. As the official contestants struggled to remember obscure facts and birding trivia, Christopher answered virtually every question in a loud stage whisper!

I last saw him at the 2006 Birdfair, when he took great pleasure in introducing what was billed as the final public appearance of the 'guvnor' of British birding, fellow Scot D.I.M. (Ian) Wallace. Seeing these two great men together on the stage reminded me just how much my generation owes to people like them, pioneers of birding at a time when it was neither as fashionable nor as popular as it is today.

SATURDAY 20 JANUARY

Cheddar Reservoir, Somerset

Given Christopher's passing, it seemed appropriate to go out birding for an hour or so, which is exactly what Nigel and I did. I decided to take him to Cheddar Reservoir, though a howling westerly gale made it very hard to do any serious birding at this exposed, blustery spot at the foot of the Mendip Hills.

I am always a bit wary of going birding with Nigel, as despite his modesty he really is one of Britain's top field birders. Now a respectable publisher, he also has a wild past: in the late 1970s he and a birding companion travelled overland by bus to India, solely in order to watch birds. Later he became one of our most experienced bird tour leaders, and has seen something approaching half the world's bird species. So I wasn't sure that an hour at Cheddar Reservoir in the middle of January would be very satisfying for him; though, as often happens, I was wrong.

As we walked along the perimeter path we saw a small gull perched on the bank, desperately trying to avoid being blown away by the fierce gusts of wind. At first I didn't give it a second glance, having assumed it was a Black-headed Gull, the commonest species here.

But Nigel is a more conscientious (and much better) birder than I am, and he looked at the bird properly, then suggested I did so too. To my astonishment, I found I was looking at a Kittiwake, a sea-going bird rarely seen inland. Presumably it had been blown in from the nearby Bristol Channel by the gales.

A useful lesson: never take anything for granted.

SATURDAY 20 JANUARY

Westhay, Somerset

In recent years, birding has become something of a spectator sport, with the birders themselves now being part of the spectacle. The crowds of people turning up at twitches, to see some wandering vagrant many miles from home, are frequently reported in the news media; while showpiece reserves such as Minsmere and Titchwell attract hundreds of thousands of visitors every year.

But a more recent phenomenon still is the arrival of equally large crowds to see Starling roosts, such as the one down the road from us at Westhay on the Somerset Levels.

I blame Bill Oddie. Ever since he went into reveries of delight at seeing the extraordinary display of roosting Starlings, his many millions of fans have wanted to share the experience. The phenomenon has become so popular that a major lager firm even bought the footage to use in one of their television adverts.

So, an hour or so before dusk on a chilly mid-winter's afternoon, we joined the throng. We'd brought quite a crowd ourselves – a bunch of friends, colleagues and their families, including our own three children, on their very first visit to the roost.

The anticipation was almost as fascinating as the event. Most people had not even brought binoculars, and were not absolutely sure what they were looking for. The first few flocks of gulls flying overhead were misidentified as Starlings, while other birds – such as singing Cetti's Warblers and a couple of Water Rails squealing noisily in the reeds – were simply ignored.

But once the action really got underway, everything else was forgotten. At 4.15 precisely, about half an hour before dusk, half a dozen compact little birds appeared in the sky overhead. They were followed by a few more, then a larger flock, and another: advance parties for the main event. The spectators stopped talking and started watching, as larger and larger flocks flew in from all points of the compass.

As the numbers began to build to plague-like proportions, we held our breath – would the birds simply drop down into the reeds, as they often do in wet or windy conditions, or would they put on their special aerial display?

Fortunately, the weather was ideal, with a bright sky in the west as the backdrop to the show. And for the next three quarters of an hour, the Starlings performed to perfection: forming vast, concentrated flocks, each containing tens of thousands of birds, swooping, turning and gyrating into extraordinary shapes. Watching them, it was hard not to think that some higher force was guiding their movements.

The truth is even more amazing: these protean, amoeba-like shapes are simply the consequence of every single bird in the flock watching its immediate neighbours and reacting to their movements. So if one bird responds to an external factor – perhaps panicking at the sight of a predator – the whole flock will follow suit. It is the tiny time delays between each bird's reactions that create these incredible patterns in the sky.

The response of the human watchers was almost as fascinating as the behaviour of the birds. Children pointed, open-mouthed, or giggled with delight as another phalanx of birds passed low over our heads. Adults, initially talkative, were hushed by the extraordinary sight of hundreds of thousands – perhaps millions – of birds.

Then, at some unseen signal, the first birds began to drop out of the bottom of the flock like water rushing down a plughole. Once they started, it was as if a switch had gone on in every single Starling's brain – a panic button telling them to find shelter as soon as they could. The trickle became a rush, then a flood, and within minutes the vast flocks were no longer airborne, but down in the reedbed, out of sight.

But not out of our hearing. Strangely, although the aerial display is completely silent, as soon as the Starlings landed in the reeds they began to chatter amongst themselves – almost as if they needed all their concentration for their aerial manoeuvres, and were now finally able to let off steam and relax.

At nightfall, as the very last birds dropped to earth, we human watchers were reduced to a reverent silence – and cold fingers and toes. Finally the straggling crocodile of people headed back to their cars, satisfied with having seen what is probably the best Starling roost in the world . . .

MONDAY 29 JANUARY – THURSDAY 1 FEBRUARY

Cairngorms, Scotland

One of the joys of birding is that wherever you are – from the heart of our cities to the remotest offshore island – there will always be birds to see.

Or so I thought, until I spent a winter's afternoon on the high tops of the Cairngorms, on a recce for a television programme I was making about Wilderness Britain. Along with my colleagues Nick and Jolie, I had taken the funicular railway up to the summit, then walked back down the mountain towards the car park, accompanied by local ecologist Cathy Mordaunt.

Despite the perfect weather conditions – blue skies, bright sunshine and only a light breeze – the birds simply failed to appear. In two hours we did not see a single sign of avian life, though we did have a highly enjoyable walk with amazing views.

In the depths of winter, there are only two species I would expect to see. A flock of Snow Buntings – the ultimate Arctic songbird – usually hangs around the restaurant at the top of the funicular railway, feeding on scraps of food dropped by visitors. But today, perhaps because of the unseasonably mild weather, they had ventured farther afield and could not be found.

The name of the catering establishment gives a clue to our main quarry. Fortunately, the Ptarmigan Restaurant doesn't actually serve up this famous grouse to its diners; but this is the one bird you would definitely expect to see here. Easily winning the contest for Britain's toughest bird, the Ptarmigan spends its whole life on these bleak, windswept mountains. Here, winds can reach speeds of over 170 miles per hour, at which point the Ptarmigan finds shelter by burrowing deep inside the snow.

Given the excellent conditions, I was surprised that we didn't see any of these beautiful, snow-white birds. Perhaps they were hiding in the gullies, or had moved to another part of the mountain. I'll be back in a month or so for a second try, so fingers crossed!

Elsewhere in the highlands, it was a similarly frustrating experience. A Dipper at Nethy Bridge briefly showed itself, but spent most of the time out of sight. A few Siskins coming to feeders in a garden were some compensation, but it was their close relative that provided the most surprising moment of the trip.

Arriving back at the Aviemore Highland Resort, a soulless collection of buildings looking like an eastern European housing development and catering to the rapidly declining skiing industry, I noticed a large flock of birds in the bushes by the car park.

A quick look through the bins (birders' slang for binoculars) revealed their identity as Lesser Redpolls, one of our most delightful (and increasingly scarce) finches. I was close enough to see their distinctive, rather stumpy shape, the short, pointed bill, and the crimson patch on the forehead of the male birds that gives the species its name. They dropped down on the grass to feed, then flew up in a cloud of flashing wings, before flitting away into the steely grey sky.

That's the funny thing about birding: you never know quite what you are going to see, or where you'll see it.

February

Wraysbury Gravel Pits and Virginia Water

On my way back home from a work meeting in London, I couldn't resist stopping off at two of my old birding haunts, Wraysbury Gravel Pits and Virginia Water. Along with Shepperton Gravel Pits and Staines Reservoirs, these were two of the main places I cut my birding teeth. Despite their proximity to London, the M25 and the Heathrow flight path, both allowed me to see species that I rarely saw elsewhere, notably two kinds of duck: Smew and Mandarin.

Having parked my car by the station at Wraysbury, I set off down the footpath that leads to Heron Lake, the most productive of these disused gravel pits.

The mild weather of the past few weeks has persisted; so much so that I felt uncomfortably warm in my thick fleece. This was a far cry from my first visits here back in the 1970s, when frost and ice were the norm rather than the exception, and my fingers and toes would soon lose all feeling.

As a result of the sunshine, a cacophony of spring sounds was in progress: Robins, Great Tits, Song Thrushes and Chaffinches competed to sing the loudest; very strange for early February. And loud screeching overhead signalled the presence of several pairs of Ring-necked Parakeets, the new kid on the block, so much commoner now than when I used to come here as a teenager.

Lost in a reverie about climate change as I wandered along, I failed to notice my main quarry – which flew off in a flurry of rapid wing-beats, its distinctive black-and-white plumage only just visible as it disappeared into the sunlit sky. It was a male Smew, which had been hiding in the vegetation at the side of the path.

I walked forward, more slowly and carefully this time, and was rewarded for my efforts. Despite a panicky flapping of wings, the next Smew I flushed settled on the other side of the water, enabling me to enjoy excellent views. I watched as he bathed and preened, waggling his tail; showing off the gorgeous subtlety of his black, white and pearl-grey plumage in the bright morning sun.

Smew truly is the most beautiful British duck. No matter how many times you see one, it always feels like a privilege. Their rarity is one factor, of course: only a couple of hundred birds spend the winter here – mostly in the south-east.

Growing up in west London, I always felt honoured that this beautiful bird would come all the way from Northern Russia to these unprepossessing gravel pits on the edge of suburbia. Perhaps if global warming really does take hold, and the Smew choose to stay in the Baltic or the Netherlands instead of crossing the North Sea, this will become an increasingly rare sight in Britain.

It occurred to me that in the thirty years or so I have been watching

Smew, I don't think I have ever seen one so close, in such good light, for so long. Finally, having finished his bath, he flew off. Soon he will head back north and east to breed somewhere in the boreal forests, nesting in a hole in a tree.

Another bird of my youth, the Great Crested Grebe, was already thinking about spring. Against the backdrop of the M25, two grebes were facing up to each other and shaking their heads, the prelude to a full-blown courtship display. Unfortunately, one or both lost interest, and the famous 'Penguin dance', in which the birds stand up in the water and wave water weed at each other, did not transpire.

As I was leaving, a couple of visiting birders asked my advice on where to go in the area. As I answered them, for the first time since leaving London it occurred to me that this was no longer my 'local patch'. Nevertheless it was great to go back and enjoy some of my favourite birds – including, of course, those noisy Ring-necked Parakeets.

When I was growing up, one of my mother's favourite walks was around the large ornamental lake at Virginia Water on the Surrey/Berkshire border. So it brought back pleasant memories to take a stroll around the lake again on this bright February morning.

The main attraction here is another duck: not a winter visitor like the Smew, but a permanent resident. Mandarin ducks were brought here in the 18th and 19th centuries from their native home in China. Like another species of ornamental waterfowl, the Canada Goose, the Mandarin rather liked its new surroundings, and today several thousand pairs breed in Britain, with its stronghold here in the Home Counties.

Nevertheless, it can be a difficult bird to see, and today was one of those days when despite searching diligently along the banks of the lake I failed to do so. While I was scanning from the stone bridge at the western end I did catch sight of a piece of litter – perhaps some wrapping discarded by a visiting picnicker – in the branches over-hanging the water.

It was only after I'd looked away that the true identity of the blue-and-orange 'wrapping' dawned on me. Sure enough, as I looked back, it turned, and revealed itself as a Kingfisher.

As often happens, it immediately dived out of sight, but soon reappeared, darting across the water like a bullet to the other bank. As a parade of pram-pushing mums, joggers and ramblers passed behind me, I wanted to yell, 'Come and see – a Kingfisher!' But, at the risk of being regarded as a nutcase, I didn't. I did, however, wonder how they could pass so close to the Kingfisher's world, and yet never come into contact with it.

The other day, a colleague of mine had asked me where she could see a Kingfisher, a question I found hard to answer. One of the joys of this gorgeous creature is that sightings are rarely predictable; seeing that unmistakable, vivid combination of cobalt blue and deep orange is always a surprise and delight.

The very first time I saw a Kingfisher was as a ten year old, back in August 1970, right here at Virginia Water. My mother and I were taking a walk through the woods around the lake when a flash of electric blue and orange caught our eye, and for a few brief seconds we watched it fly past. I can still remember thinking 'but what a tiny little bird!' – barely larger than a sparrow. With some birds, that sense of joy and wonder never goes away, and it's always a good day when you see a Kingfisher.

My reverie was interrupted by what I took to be the mooing of a distant cow, but then realised was a chainsaw. I've obviously got used to living in the countryside. I waited for another sighting of the Kingfisher, but in vain. And soon it was time to head back to the car park, the A303, and home.

Perhaps that's how birding should be – always leaving you wanting a little more . . .

Cheddar Reservoir

With children's birthday parties, the participants are often left short-tempered, exhausted and tearful – and that's just the parents. So after two-year-old George and Daisy's hectic celebration, I needed a spot of fresh air; and a visit to Cheddar Reservoir, a few miles to the north of my home, was the perfect solution.

I like reservoirs. Their very artificiality is, for me, their strong point. Where else do you find a habitat with such perfect all-round visibility? And when, as at Cheddar, there is a convenient footpath around the entire perimeter, there isn't really any excuse for missing a bird.

Or so you might imagine. In fact, even on a reservoir as compact as Cheddar, where with a telescope you can easily see to the far side, birds are easy to miss. It took me three or four visits before I finally caught up with the little flock of Scaup that have spent the winter here, and although I usually see the wintering Great Northern Diver, even this huge and prominent bird can be surprisingly elusive.

As well as a good variety of duck, and up to four thousand Coots, Cheddar Reservoir is well-known in the area for its winter gull roost. Today I arrived at just the right time – about an hour and a half before dusk – as thousands of gulls converged on the water from every direction. Most were Black-headed Gulls, though as the evening drew in, over a thousand Lesser Black-backed Gulls joined the throng. As they came in, they landed on the water and bathed, preening their feathers in order to restore cleanliness and good order.

One unfortunate bird was unable to do so. As I reached the yacht club, almost at the end of my circuit of the reservoir, I noticed a dark individual perched on an offshore raft. It was a Black-headed Gull, whose plumage was sullied with a sickly yellow hue – the tell-tale stains of oil on its feathers. It could fly, but not very well, and I fear that it will suffer the fate of almost all oiled birds – a slow and lingering death.

Unlike my visit here back in January, when a howling gale was blowing, today conditions were windless; though there was another unusual bird to be seen. A Mediterranean Gull – possibly the same one I saw over the garden a few weeks ago – was sitting on the water surrounded by its commoner relatives. Swimming, it was harder to identify than when in flight, but the combination of pale wingtips, plus the deep red bill and dark face-mask, confirmed its identity.

For some birders, gull identification is one of the most fascinating aspects of their hobby; others ignore them, lumping them together as mere 'seagulls'. I sit somewhere between these two camps: while I can think of many more beautiful and fascinating birds, gulls do combine identification challenges with interesting behaviour. Even as it grew too dark to see, I could still enjoy the murmuring sounds of several thousand gulls as they prepared for a night's sleep.

TUESDAY 27 FEBRUARY

Cairngorms

We have returned to the top of the Cairngorms, but this time two things have changed. First, I have come with a film crew, and presenter Alan Titchmarsh, to film the opening sequence for our programme on wilderness habitats for the forthcoming BBC One series *The Nature of Britain*. Second, the mild, sunny conditions have been replaced by a blizzard. Fortunately, the aim of the sequence is to show just how harsh conditions are up here for people and wildlife, so in one sense the weather is ideal.

*

In fact the wind was so strong, and the visibility so bad, that it was surprising we could see each other, let alone any birds. And indeed my sum total of species seen on two trips up the mountain came to a paltry one: after failing to trouble the scorers last time, I redeemed my reputation amongst my colleagues by spotting two hardy Snow Buntings feeding just outside the windows of the summit restaurant. They were well camouflaged: mainly white, with patches of brown and grey which helped to break up their outline, making them surprisingly hard to spot amongst the snow and rocks.

Snow Buntings are truly incredible creatures. No other small bird anywhere in the world can survive in such harsh weather conditions. This is more or less the southernmost edge of their global range, as they breed well to the north, in Scandinavia, Iceland and the Arctic – although in winter small flocks do gather as far south as East Anglia. They are the only songbird – and one of just three species in total – which has been seen at the North Pole itself.

We are used to regarding Snow Buntings as a bird of the high mountains, at least during the breeding season. Yet when I visited Iceland with Bill Oddie a few years ago, I remember hearing an unusual song as we collected our hire car at Reykjavik Airport. Looking up, I was astonished by the unmistakable sight of a male Snow Bunting in full song-flight – virtually at sea level. I stood watching it, open-mouthed, as it launched itself from its perch, then winnowed the air on fluttering wings before returning to the earth.

I had forgotten a basic rule of plant and animal distribution: that as you travel farther north, so high altitude species are found at lower levels. In Iceland the Snow Bunting – given the delightful name of Snjótittlingur (pronounced 'snow-tit-ling-er') – is a garden bird, as we discovered when we visited the tiny island of Flatey.

After a couple of days, even we were finding the bird's tinkling song just a wee bit monotonous, though perhaps that was more to do with the virtual absence of other songbirds rather than the Snow Bunting itself.

When I got home from our Scottish trip, I dug out one of my favourite bird books, Desmond Nethersole-Thompson's monograph of the Snow Bunting. Nethersole-Thompson was an extraordinary character, who bridged the divide between the Victorian collectors and the modern birders. Having begun as a devout egg collector, he later turned his nest-finding skills to good use by becoming one of our greatest ever field ornithologists.

His commitment to his studies bordered on the obsessional, as *The Snow Bunting* reveals. Having given up his teaching job and headed north, he and his wife Carrie decided to live in a tent on the very top of the Cairngorm plateau, in order to study the Snow Buntings at first hand.

In one of my favourite passages from the book, Nethersole-Thompson recalls just how bad the conditions were:

> A July cloudburst nearly washed us out. Water ran off the hills and poured like a burn right through the tent. Clothes, blankets, and bread were wet and sodden . . . We huddled close in misery and growing hopelessness. How eagerly we welcomed the first greyness of dawn, although outside the mist was grey and clinging. Then, almost like a miracle, the mist vanished; and by noon we had begun to dry out.
>
> Sometimes big winds blew up in the night . . . The small tent often seemed about to rise and fly, but somehow it always held. For whole weeks the wind roared against the canvas, dulling our wits and condemning us to passive inactivity . . . We lost count of days – each often seemed more miserable than the one before – and had to shout against the roar of the wind.

Later on, the couple even took their infant son Brock up the mountain, stuffed into a bag designed for carrying shot game!

Another son, Des, also became a fine naturalist. Last summer he helped my colleagues film Dotterel for the *Nature of Britain* series, on the same high tops where his father and mother had spent so much time studying Scotland's birds.

March

SUNDAY 4 MARCH

Catcott Lows, Burtle Road and Tealham Moor, Somerset

It was a rainy afternoon, but as we had visitors we decided to take a drive over to Catcott and visit the hide there. Unfortunately, despite my confident assertion that the rain would be coming from the west, I was wrong; a full-blown easterly was blowing squally showers and wind right through the hide windows.

Not a good place to bring three-year-old Charlie for one of his first birding experiences, so after briefly scanning the flocks of duck we got back into the car and headed home, taking the scenic route via Burtle Road Lakes and Tealham Moor.

Just as I was saying that the fields alongside the lakes might be a good place for Little Egrets, we ran into a flock of them. Thirteen of these glorious, snow-white birds were feeding in a field to the side of the road. Disturbed briefly as we stopped, they simply flew over our heads and into the adjacent field, giving us excellent views despite the rain. After taking our fill of the spectacle, we drove home across Tealham Moor, counting a further eight egrets – and over 140 Mute Swans – along the way.

TUESDAY 6 MARCH

Mill Batch

A fine, sunny morning at the start of March brought a welcome change in the weather, after what felt like weeks of miserable rain. As the sun warmed up the more sheltered corners of the garden, the first butterflies of the year began to appear. A Small Tortoiseshell flew past the kitchen window, and later on I saw a Brimstone, resplendent in his fresh, lemon-yellow colours. For the first time this year, it really did feel like spring.

Not surprisingly, the songbirds were also out in force. On an early morning stroll down the garden I was serenaded by Wren, Song Thrush, Dunnock, Robin and Great Tit. But the loudest sound didn't come from a songbird, but from the most sociable member of the crow family, the Rook. The line of ash trees at the bottom of the garden holds at least a dozen Rook's nests, and the birds chatter incessantly amongst themselves from dawn to dusk.

The Rook is the quintessential bird of the British countryside. Ten thousand years ago, before humans began to farm the land, Rooks were almost certainly unknown in Britain. But as woodland was cleared for farming, Rooks spread westwards across Europe by following the plough. Today there are more than a million pairs breeding in Britain and Ireland – well over one third of the European population.

Like all members of the crow family, Rooks have given rise to their fair share of folklore. Ancient beliefs include the idea that they form a 'parliament' to judge and condemn their fellow birds; and the widely-held notion that a rookery on your land brings good luck – a notion that rather appeals to me.

Indeed, many of the words and sayings attributed to crows actually apply to Rooks – notably 'as the crow flies', referring to the direct flight-lines Rooks will follow to and from their roosting sites. Even the word 'scarecrow' is a misnomer, the effigy having been invented to ward off marauding flocks of Rooks rather than the solitary Carrion Crow.

It is perhaps not surprising that the Rook and Carrion Crow are often confused; though with practice it is easy to spot the Rook's looser, more shambling flight. Given close views, the Rook's bare, greyish face-patch is also obvious.

Rooks are amongst the earliest birds to breed, and ours are no exception. For the past few weeks they have been making repairs to last year's nests, bringing back twigs which they weave into a loose assembly, to which they will soon entrust their precious eggs. This morning I noticed a pair in the next door farmyard, the male fanning out his glossy blue-black plumage and displaying to the female – who promptly flew away, unimpressed.

Each evening, the sound of the Rooks changes tone, with a greater sense of urgency than earlier in the day. Numbers build up too, with birds returning to the rookery, until the twigs are bending beneath their weight. Just before dusk, they begin to fly south in small groups, presumably heading to a nearby roost. Finally, the last couple of birds leave, and for the first time since sunrise, the garden falls silent.

Saltholme RSPB Reserve, Teesside

In the spare couple of hours before I was due to give a talk in Newcastle-upon-Tyne, I was given a sneak preview of what is set to become the RSPB's flagship reserve in the north of England, Saltholme, situated on the north bank of the River Tees near Middlesbrough.

As we approached, I could see that this was going to be a great place to watch birds. Why? Because it felt like I'd reached the ends of the earth. All around, the legacy of heavy industry was evident: smoking chimneys, steel structures and acres of what, to the untrained eye, would generally appear to be 'wasteland'. Wildlife loves these sorts of places – mainly, I suspect, because people don't. Abandoned sites draw birds like a magnet, and this one was no exception.

I was given a guided tour by Kevin Bayes, the RSPB's project manager for the site. As he explained, his job involves everything from planning where the best wader habitat will be, to designing the kitchen for the visitor centre café. A local man, his passion for this place and its birds is obvious in all he says and does. Vision is everything: the vision to see that a derelict industrial site can be transformed – with the help of a few million pounds – into a must-see attraction for families from all over the north of England.

Being a hardcore birder, Kevin is determined not to alienate his fellow enthusiasts, many of whom have been finding rarities on this site for years. Fortunately, with over 1000 acres available, both the birding community and general public can be accommodated. While the families can gaze out from the comfort of the visitor centre, the serious birders can wander to the farthest corners of the reserve, and get suitably cold and wet.

As the wind whipped in from the Tees estuary, we took a stroll around. The shallow pools are, as you would expect, excellent for wildfowl, with a nice selection of dabbling duck including Wigeon, Teal and Gadwall; and a pair of displaying Ruddy Ducks.

The surrounding grassy fields echoed to the song of Skylarks – a welcome change from my home in Somerset where this iconic farm-land bird is now so scarce. A croaking call and a rapid whirring of wings alerted us to two Grey Partridges – a bird which has now almost vanished from my part of the world – while overhead, two Peregrines tussled with the local crows. Change is inevitable in the bird world, so while it saddened me to be reminded that so many farmland birds have declined in recent years, the sight of these magnificent raptors in full flow gladdened my heart.

In a year or two, Saltholme will open its doors to visitors; a decade later, it will be as well-known to RSPB members as Minsmere or Titchwell. It is a tribute to people like Kevin that places like this con-tinue to be created for the enjoyment of tens of thousands of visitors. I look forward to coming back soon.

TUESDAY 13 MARCH

Mill Batch and Cheddar Reservoir

The other day my son Charlie noticed a flattened strip of grass on our back lawn, and I patiently explained to him that this was made by a large, black-and-white animal which only comes out at night. He paused for a moment, put his head to one side and enquirted: 'Was it a Zebra?'

Having explained to him that the creature involved was more likely to be a Badger, he was keen to get out this morning to see if any more trails had been made overnight. So just before I headed off for work, we took a stroll down the garden. No Badgers, but we did hear the unmistakable sound of a Chiffchaff, shouting his name for all the world to hear. Newly returned from Africa, and keen to attract a mate, he was easy to see as he flitted around in the twigs at the base of our large ash tree.

Meanwhile a splendid cock Blackbird sung from a post, and nearby, three Dunnocks (presumably two males and a female) chased each other around our elder bush. I went to work filled with the joys of the spring season to come.

Coming home as the sun set, I made a brief diversion to Cheddar Reservoir, in the hope of catching up with two rare winter visitors from the north. Iceland and Glaucous Gulls are birds of the Arctic, but in winter a few of them head south to Britain, where they may turn up almost anywhere with their commoner relatives.

As I climbed up to the path that runs around the reservoir rim, I saw a small huddle of fellow birders about a hundred yards away, scanning the gull roost with a battery of telescopes. I sidled up and ascertained that despite having been there since half past four (by now it was gone six) they had so far drawn a blank.

The gulls – mainly Lesser Black-backed, with a few Herring, Common and Black-headed – were gathering on the water across the other side of the reservoir, so my telescope was essential. Just as I was scanning the flock, I heard the call we all wanted to hear: 'There's the Iceland!'

A moment of comical frustration ensued, as we tried to follow the finder's directions: 'In front of the white house. No, not that one, the one with the gazebo. Near the trees; no not those trees, *these* trees . . .' Eventually we all fixed on the correct spot, and a strikingly pale gull with no black at all on the wingtips swam into view. Satisfied sighs all round.

A minute or two later, and another call: 'Glaucous. Well to the left.' Another frantic scan; another, much larger, bird with a plumage the colour of a Rich Tea biscuit. Glaucous Gull in the bag.

With eight kinds of gull at Cheddar this year, it's been a good run; though I still have some catching up to do with one local birder, Bruce Taylor, who has seen no fewer than 14 different species in east Somerset in the past year or so. Those of you who didn't realise there are as many as 14 different kinds of gull in Britain – and those of you who don't really care – will probably not be impressed, but believe me, this is quite an achievement!

Countess Wear, near Exeter, Devon

Gulls are famous for their inappropriate names. Black-headed Gulls have brown hoods; Mediterranean Gulls live all over Europe; Common Gulls are not especially common. But the prize for the least apt moniker must go to the Laughing Gull of North America. There's something about its profile – a lugubrious expression enhanced by a drooping bill and dark, heavily-lidded eyes – that always makes it look rather miserable.

Laughing Gull has long been one of my British 'bogey birds' – a species I would have expected to have seen here by now, but never have. Although hailing from the eastern seaboard of North America, they are a fairly regular visitor to our shores; and when they do come, they often stay put for long periods, making them relatively easy to see. Nevertheless, although I have seen thousands of them in the US, I have yet to catch up with one in Britain.

Last year I heard that a Laughing Gull was overwintering in the unlikely surroundings of the Madejski Stadium on the outskirts of Reading. It was known to spend most of its time outside the local McDonald's, where eager twitchers kept it fed on Happy Meals and Big Macs. I did pop in on my way to Bristol one day, but the bird had obviously decided to go for a healthier diet elsewhere.

So when another Laughing Gull turned up on the outskirts of Exeter this month, I just had to go. As the site was less than an hour's drive down the M5, I decided to give Charlie a taste of twitching – if only to put him off. He made the sensible decision to fall asleep somewhere around Taunton, and failed to wake up even when I stopped the car by the busy road junction where the gull was rumoured to be.

Normally, twitches are frustrating affairs: I usually arrive moments after the bird has flown, to be met by a group of smug birders comparing notes – or worse still, nowadays, showing you pictures of the recently-departed bird on their mobile phones and digital cameras. This time, luck was on my side. Although my directions were fairly vague, I did notice a suitable patch of watery habitat to my right, and managed to park in a lay-by on the opposite side of the road.

Lifting my binoculars, the very first bird I saw had the tell-tale dark plumage and long, drooping bill of a Laughing Gull. A quick check with my telescope confirmed its identity, and the 371st bird I had seen in Britain (or thereabouts – I gave up keeping a proper British list several years ago) was duly ticked off.

As with all twitches to see a rare bird, there was the usual mixture of relief and anticlimax. The fact that I have also seen Laughing Gulls frequently in their native home, and that not even the most ardent gull enthusiast would describe this bird as beautiful, meant that I didn't plan to hang around for long. After a few minutes, the bird made up my mind for me: taking off, it flew into the distance on long, loose wings.

Charlie woke up when we reached Exeter Services. There, over a chocolate muffin and fruit smoothie, I carefully explained that we had already been birding, and that now we were on our way home. He didn't seem terribly disappointed.

MONDAY 19 MARCH

Mill Batch

Having written about our garden Rooks in my Birdwatch column in the *Guardian*, I received the following e-mail from a reader:

Dear Stephen Moss

Enjoyed your piece on Rooks in today's Guardian. Not nearly enough bird coverage in the paper for my liking, considering how big a part of so many people's lives birds are.

To take issue with you on one thing – you call Carrion Crows 'solitary', and of course they almost always are, at least in rural areas. But here in west London I regularly see big assemblages of crows, at low water on the Thames shore and in the Wetland Centre. Fifty or sixty together is not an unusual sight, and they do seem to act like genuine flocks – feeding together and taking off as a group (though I have no evidence of colonial nesting). Have they become the 'urban Rook'? And why are there no urban Rooks, when most cities contain substantial stretches of open country in the shape of parks? It's not as if Rooks are choosy – I've seen them robbing the rubbish bins at motorway service stations.

George Chamier

It's a fair point – I know there used to be 'semi-urban' Rooks – at least in Richmond Park on the outskirts of London, though nowadays only Carrion Crows and Jackdaws are found there.

FRIDAY 23 MARCH

Whiteladies Road, Bristol

Those of us who work at the BBC in Bristol are fortunate that, when the founders of the Natural History Unit set up shop here half a century ago, they chose to base themselves in one of the city's leafier suburbs, on the borders of Clifton, Cotham and Redland.

As a result, we regularly enjoy a morning and evening chorus of birdsong. From late March onwards, Blackcaps, Chiffchaffs and a host of other songbirds are standard fare, while Sparrowhawks often patrol overhead. Coming home from a Christmas party one year, I was serenaded by a Wren, stimulated by the security lights to sing at two a.m. on a frosty December night.

Occasionally something rarer passes by: such as the Red Kite seen by the editor of *The Natural World*, or the flock of Waxwings that had the bad timing to turn up in the car park when I was away on location.

While parking my car on a Friday morning in March, I heard a distinctive, two-note call – reminiscent of one of the Great Tit's varied repertoire of tunes, but subtly different. Looking up into one of the large, mature trees overhanging the car park, I noticed a compact little bird with a pleasing combination of brown, buffs and blacks in its plumage, and a distinctive white patch on the back of its neck: a Coal Tit.

Coal Tits are not your usual city fare, but the number of trees and bushes in the area, many of which are the coniferous variety preferred by this species, means there are a few pairs here in the heart of Bristol.

What happened next was a real surprise. The Coal Tit flew low over my head, and nipped into a tiny crack in the stone wall by the exit to the car park. I can only presume that the bird, which normally makes its home in holes or cracks in trees, was prospecting a nest site. Hopefully, over the next few weeks, I shall find out whether it plans to make its nest here.

[Postscript: It didn't!]

SATURDAY 24 MARCH

Mill Batch

Spring is a funny season. It teases you with warm, sunny days, full of promise. Yet there is also a sense of frustration, as you wait for that promise to be delivered. Despite seeing my first butterflies more than two weeks ago, insect activity has been almost non-existent since; and though I had high hopes of today, with temperatures nudging 12 or 13 degrees, the butterflies have failed to appear – perhaps put off by a chilly edge to the wind.

Still, the Chiffchaff in the willows reminds me that spring is just around the corner. This neat little bird may not be all that much to look at – basically olive-green with a paler eyestripe – and he may not sing as well as other members of his family. But his relentless cheery 'chiff-chiff-chaff-chiff-chaff', which if I strain my ears I can hear from the back door, fills me with anticipation for the months ahead.

Later that day, a flock of about 70 Golden Plover flew over, their pale plumage glinting in the afternoon sunshine. A lovely reminder that the birds were here long before we were – and that the Somerset Levels, despite all the many changes, is still a primitive landscape where birds can find sanctuary from the modern world.

SUNDAY 25 MARCH

Cheddar Reservoir

Birders – especially those with families – must take their chances when they can. So when I found I had half an hour to spare before Sunday lunch, I couldn't resist dashing up to Cheddar Reservoir to twitch a rare American duck, the Lesser Scaup.

Size apart, there is nothing particularly 'lesser' about this rather fine-looking duck. And though it is quite common in North America, it is a real rarity over this side of the Atlantic, with only a handful of accepted records. So although I don't always go chasing after every rare bird I hear about, its proximity to my home allowed me to make an exception.

As I walked up the path to the reservoir, my heart sank. I had forgotten that it was Sunday, so the local yacht club was out in force. In fact their presence made it much easier for me, as I soon realised. Virtually all the birds, including large numbers of gulls, about 60 Great Crested Grebes, and flocks of ducks, had been pushed over towards the near bank, which meant they were all much easier to see.

It didn't take me long to find the Lesser Scaup: all I needed was to scan along the bank until I saw a huddle of birders clustered around their telescopes like a prayer meeting of some minor religious sect.

I joined them, and trained my optics on the group of ducks floating on the water just a few yards offshore. I couldn't have hoped for better views: not just of the target bird itself, but also a quartet of its commoner and larger relative, Greater Scaup.

Getting the two male birds side by side was particularly instructive, the slimmer and less stocky shape marking out the rarer bird. The plumage differences were, to the untrained eye, fairly minimal; though experienced birders present pointed out the slightly darker tinge to the vermiculations (posh word for the stripy grey pattern) on the Lesser Scaup's back. Otherwise both species sport a black head, neck and breast, snowy-white flanks and a black rear-end.

Birders take great pleasure in noticing tiny variations in the shape, structure and plumage of a rare bird: in this case, the slight peak to the back of the head. To me, the bright yellow eye – a feature it shares with several of its commoner relatives – was equally striking.

At least no one was disputing this particular bird's identity. The problem with 'diving ducks' (of the genus *Aythya*, for those of you with a scientific bent) is that they hybridise more frequently, and in more different combinations, than virtually any other wild bird. I had nearly been caught out by this last Christmas, when I found what I thought was another American rarity, a Ring-necked Duck, on nearby Burtle Road Lakes.

It was only when I returned home and made a final double-check in the Collins' Field Guide that I realised that I had been watching a Pochard x Tufted Duck hybrid, which closely resembles the rare species.

As Edmund Blackadder once drawled, on hearing a particularly lengthy anecdote, 'The long winter nights must simply fly by . . .' Yet birders love this sort of abstruse identification puzzle, and will happily discuss it for hours . . .

TUESDAY 27 MARCH

Mill Batch

Once a week I try to spend a morning – sometimes even a whole day – working at home, catching up on the endless torrent of e-mails. Today, by about four p.m., I could stand it no more, and took a quiet stroll down the garden. A stiff breeze concealed the fact that the temperature was really quite warm; certainly warm enough for Peacock, Small Tortoiseshell and Comma butterflies to emerge and test their wings. And at the end of the garden, there was a lovely surprise: a single Long-tailed Tit which perched on the brambles just long enough for me to get a close-up view.

I wonder if they will nest here this year . . .

FRIDAY 30 MARCH

Mill Batch

Nana and Grandpa are here, so the children are happy.

Grandpa and two-year-old George spent the morning looking out of the back window and naming the birds. Just as every colour for George is blue, so every bird he sees is a Blue Tit. Or so I thought, until

Grandpa pointed out that George really can identify Blue Tits – or at least tell them apart from the other birds visiting the feeder.

I tested his identification skills with a photograph of a Blue Tit, and he passed with flying colours. I am proud beyond belief, and can't wait until he is old enough to debate abstruse identification points of the larger gulls, or discuss the subsong of the Blackcap.

But whenever I mention birds to George's twin sister Daisy, she looks at me with a mixture of pity and amusement. I fear she already realises that birding is not very cool.

The American way of birding . . .

The editor of *Ibis*, the prestigious journal of the British Ornithologists' Union, has sent me a book to review. Unlike other magazines, *Ibis* doesn't pay a fee – the prestige alone is considered to be enough inducement. Which, given that the journal is almost 150 years old, it is.

The book is by an author I have only vaguely heard of, Marjorie Valentine Adams. Now in her nineties, she is one of the last living links to the golden age of American birding – the era between the two world wars in which the pastime was dragged out of the era of shooting and collecting, and into the modern age.

The title, *Bird-Witched: How Birds Can Change a Life*, rather put me off, but I persisted and, despite the author's rather twee, homely style, was eventually rewarded. Her encounters with the legendary Roger Tory Peterson – author and illustrator of the original *Field Guide to the Birds* – made fascinating reading. Apparently Peterson, unlike most other great birders, was an owl rather than a lark. He compensated for his inability to rise early by staying up all night working, then nipping outside for an hour to experience the dawn chorus before retiring to bed.

In the final chapter, Adams tells the most fascinating story of all:

how she and her late husband saved the Arizonan breeding grounds of one of America's rarest warblers – the Golden-cheeked – from disappearing under suburban sprawl. The irony is that once the warbler's breeding grounds had been safeguarded for the future, the poor people who actually owned the land, on which they depended for an income in retirement, found that it had become almost worthless.

I am also rereading *Kingbird Highway*, by Kenn Kaufman, one of today's leading American birders. It is one of those books that creep up on you; the outcome being more satisfying than you expect when you begin.

Subtitled 'The Biggest Year in the Life of an Extreme Birder', it chronicles an intensive year's birding back in the early 1970s. The author – then a fresh-faced and naïve 18 year old who had flunked out of high school – pursued the ultimate American birder's dream of seeing more species in North America in a single calendar year than anyone else.

What makes the book so much better than most 'birder's tales' is that Kaufman waited more than thirty years, until he reached middle age, to write down the story. As a result we see the youth through the older man's eyes, with the benefit of both hindsight and perspective:

> In the early 1970s, we were not birdwatching. We were *birding*, and that made all the difference. We were out to see, to discover, to chase, to learn, to find as many different kinds of bird as possible – and, in friendly competition, to try to find more of them than the next birder. We became a *community* of birders, with the complications that human societies always have; and although it was the birds that had brought us together, our story became a human story after all.

Having spent an eventful year on the road, with the highs and lows, ups and downs, great sightings and frustrating misses, the boy finally became a man – with a very different attitude to life. He had broken the record, but this didn't seem to matter any more – after all, someone would come along and break it again soon.

In the closing chapter, following a near-death experience, Kaufman realises that he has been so obsessed with *listing* the birds he hasn't really been *looking* at them. As a metaphor for the way birders live – or at least the way we would like to live – his new way of seeing the world takes some beating:

> Now, when I look back many years later, as though from a great distance, I can still see that young man standing out on the jetty. And at least on my better days, I can see myself standing there with him: shaken by experience, perhaps, but still confident that the light will be better, that the birds will come in closer, that we will see everything more clearly at last, before the day is over.

April

Dundee, Scotland

On BBC Breakfast, weather forecaster Carol Kirkwood could hardly believe her eyes. With an incredulity that only someone brought up in that fine country can muster, she announced that the east coast of Scotland would see unseasonably high temperatures today. The mercury was set to reach a scorching 20 degrees in . . . yes, I heard it right the first time . . . Dundee.

So it's official. For a brief moment in a month that broke weather records galore, Dundee was the warmest place in Britain. Good news for cameraman Steve Phillipps and myself as we set forth from the quayside hotel to film the city's most famous resident, the Red Squirrel. This was for an episode from the BBC One series *The Nature of Britain*, looking at the ecology and wildlife of our towns and cities. It gave me the opportunity to set aside birds for a day or two and concentrate on arguably Britain's most delightful mammal.

Due to an accident of geography, Dundee is now the only British city that can boast resident Red Squirrels in its parks and gardens. While the rest of us have to make do with that brash North American import, the Grey Squirrel, the good people of the city by the Tay can enjoy the antics of its native red cousin.

In fact it's the River Tay that is proving to be one of the final lines of defence against the greys. Having been brought to Britain back in the late 19th century, it's taken them over 100 years to get this far, and they are poised to make the leap across the river at any moment.

Indeed as our guide and expert helper Ken Neil, from Dundee Red Squirrel Project, pointed out, a few greys have already reached the city centre. Controversially (though in my opinion quite rightly) the Red Squirrel Project has a zero tolerance approach to the greys, using a variety of methods to 'control' (i.e. kill) them.

While those of us in the south might as well enjoy watching our city greys, here it's quite different. If nothing is done, within 10 to 15 years the greys will have taken over completely, and Dundee's Red Squirrels will have disappeared forever.

Today, as natural history film-makers, we have had the privilege of watching – and filming – the reds, mostly in glorious dappled sunlight as they foraged for food around the grounds of a hospital.

Later we visited friends of Ken's, to try to get even closer shots of the Red Squirrels. Jimmie and Rosie live on the outskirts of the city, and their house backs onto a birch wood – home to a good population of reds. Rosie is completely bed-bound through illness, so Jimmie has redesigned the house to give her the best view possible of the garden and its wildlife.

We sat in Rosie's bedroom and watched as Steve put up a small portable hide, then settled down to film the animals. Right on cue, one appeared, seized a few nuts from the feeder and ran away – but not before Steve had grabbed some stunning close-ups.

Jimmie and Rosie have become so involved with the Red Squirrel Project that Jimmie now produces an annual calendar of his photographs of these fascinating animals, the proceeds of which go towards funding the project.

After spending an hour or two in the company of our genial and selfless hosts, while enjoying amazing views of our most charming native mammal, we had more than enough material for our film. It was also good to see how getting close to wildlife can bring joy to people's lives, even in the most challenging circumstances.

EASTER WEEKEND (FRIDAY 6 – MONDAY 9 APRIL)

Mill Batch

For a few weeks now, since the middle of March, I have been hearing Chiffchaffs on my travels. Now, by Easter weekend, they are everywhere, including our back garden. On good days we can even hear them from the house.

Apart from their distinctive sound, Chiffchaffs are fairly nondescript, retiring birds. However, at this time of year, before all the leaves are back on the trees, you do stand a reasonable chance of seeing them. So as I wandered down the back lawn, listening to that classic 'chiff-chiff-chaff-chiff-chaff' sound, I kept my eyes peeled for the slightest movement.

Then I saw it: a compact little bird, olive-green in colour, and paler below, with a noticeable eyestripe. As I got closer I could also see its dark legs and relatively short wings.

The shortness of the wings is one feature that distinguishes the Chiffchaff from its close relative, the Willow Warbler. The difference in length is entirely due to their migratory habits: while Chiffchaffs mostly spend the winter around the western Mediterranean, Willow Warblers travel all the way to southern Africa, so need longer wings to complete that epic journey.

Another way to tell them apart is the date on which the first birds arrive. This year I had to wait until a sunny day in the middle of April before hearing our first Willow Warbler – a full month later than his relative. I was doing some spring-cleaning when I heard it coming from our front garden: a melodious and plaintive tune, the notes descending the scale to create a pleasing sound to the human ear. Compared with the Chiffchaff's rather tuneless ditty it is like a virtuoso musician in the presence of a novice. It also makes me realise that spring has finally arrived.

THURSDAY 12 APRIL

Cheddar Reservoir

A calm but cloudy morning seemed the perfect opportunity to drop in at Cheddar Reservoir on my way to work for half an hour's peace and quiet between children and meetings. It was a good call, as our American friends would say.

Though I was too late for the bulk of the gulls, which presumably depart their roost soon after dawn, a group of 50 or so were bathing out on the glassy surface of the water. Amongst the usual Herrings and Lesser Black-backs, there was a much larger bird, its thick white neck gleaming in the morning light, and contrasting with its sooty-black upperparts. It was our largest gull (and indeed the biggest of all the world's 50 or so gull species): a Great Black-backed.

In a nice moment of symmetry, it was then joined by the world's smallest gull, fluttering over the water like a tern on buoyant wings. Little Gulls are one of my favourite spring migrants, passing through Britain on their way to the Low Countries and Scandinavia to breed, and stopping off, like this bird, for an hour or two before continuing on their journey. Through my binoculars I could see the rounded, pale grey upperwings contrasting with the dark, smoky underwings; and through the telescope the difference was even more marked.

The warm, still morning was also perfect for one of my favourite spring events: the courtship display of the Great Crested Grebe. Pairs of grebes were scattered all over the reservoir, facing up to each other and waggling their crests in a pleasing symmetry. One bird had picked up some water weed in its bill, and was offering it to the other much as a human suitor might present a bunch of flowers or box of chocolates. Sadly, his romantic gesture went unrequited, as his mate lost interest and turned away.

Near the bank to my left, the two Great Northern Divers which have spent the winter here were gliding along; for once not even bothering to dive. These stunning birds are a rare sight in southern Britain; especially at this time of year, when I would expect them to be heading north to the Arctic to breed. In winter plumage, they look rather like a pale, fat Cormorant – and indeed are roughly the same length as that species, but about twice the weight.

All the local birders – including me – are hoping they will stay long enough to moult into their splendid breeding garb of jet black, silver and white. However, we suspect that they will probably head off in the next few days – especially now the summer weather seems to have arrived . . .

FRIDAY 13 APRIL

Wood Lane Sand and Gravel Quarry, Ellesmere, Shropshire; Catcott Lows

A hike up the M5 and M6 found me at a sand and gravel quarry in the heart of Shropshire. My own quarry was Sand Martins: one of the largest and most impressive colonies I have ever seen.

I was in the company of John Hawkins, one of the many unsung heroes of wildlife conservation in Britain. A keen birder for a good half century, John went from a childhood obsession with egg-collecting (something he shares with most of his generation) to an adult obsession with photographing birds.

Tutored by the great Eric Hosking, the original bird photographer, John gave up his trade as a butcher six years ago to pursue his passion full-time. He also runs projects for Shropshire Wildlife Trust, including the restored gravel pits at the Ellesmere quarry. He is one of those fine examples of someone for whom 'retirement' means almost constant work . . .

Last year John helped my colleague Steve Phillipps to film the Sand Martins, capturing some wonderful slow-motion shots of the birds as they flew in and out of their nests. Having enjoyed the resulting footage – and edited it into a sequence for the final programme in the *Nature of Britain* series – I really wanted to see the place for myself.

I certainly wasn't disappointed. The colony – numbering 200 or so individual nest holes – is on the sheer face of a cliff of red sand, now almost petrified into a sandstone mountain. The owners of the quarry had the foresight not to disturb the sand when the birds first colonised a few years ago, and now the colony is permanent.

As we arrived, the twittering above my head signalled the synchronised arrival of dozens of these charming little birds. At this early stage in the season they were doing the spring-cleaning: clearing out dirt and debris from their nest holes before settling down to the serious business of raising a brood of chicks – hopefully two broods if the weather stays fine.

Sand Martins are the smallest of the swallow family to breed in Britain, and also by far the earliest to arrive, probably because they spend the winter in western rather than southern Africa, so don't have quite so far to fly to get here. Nevertheless, for a bird weighing about half an ounce to fly several thousand miles, cross the Sahara

Desert, Mediterranean Sea and much of Western Europe, and arrive safely here in a remote corner of England, is still one of nature's miracles.

On my way home, I couldn't resist a swift diversion, to the hide at Catcott Lows. The view, which in winter was all water and ducks, is now a lot less water and a lot fewer ducks. But what the assembled cast may lack in quantity at this time of year, it occasionally makes up for in quality.

Amongst the usual Teal, Shoveler and Wigeon was a handsome male duck: marginally larger than a Teal, but just as compact. For a bird whose colours are basically brown, white and grey, this really was a handsome creature. The chocolate-brown head was set off by a broad, creamy-white stripe running back from the eye to the nape, and he sported silver-grey flanks, with a subtle, mottled pattern, and long, plumed feathers on his back. He was a fine drake Garganey – my first here in Somerset.

He was feeding avidly in the shallow, vegetated water – avidly, because unlike other British ducks the Garganey is a summer visitor, and he had only just arrived back from Africa. Why Garganeys head south when the rest of the duck family stay put is a bit of a mystery – but one well known to our ancestors, who referred to the bird as the 'summer teal'.

Joining me in the hide was Brian Gibbs, stalwart of the Somerset Ornithological Society and one of the leading county birders. We had a slightly depressing conversation about all the birds that should be in Somerset but are no longer commonly found here: Turtle Doves, Spotted Flycatchers and Ring Ouzels, to name but three.

With a lifetime's experience, Brian was able to take the long view, pointing out the recent arrival of new species such as Dartford Warbler up on the Mendips, and Little Egret down on the Levels, not to mention the upsurge in raptor numbers in the past couple of decades. I agree with him, but nevertheless would give a lot to be cast back fifty years in time, when the birds we have since lost were found on every moor and heath, or in every copse and hedgerow.

Shapwick and Meare Heaths, Somerset

Despite their name, these so-called 'heaths' are in fact former peat diggings turned into an extensive wetland with reedbeds, pools and little patches of scrub. Like so much of the Somerset Levels, this creates a landscape more like reclaimed areas of the Netherlands, or parts of Eastern Europe, than southern England.

With only a couple of hours early on a Sunday morning, I was a little disappointed to wake to thick morning mist, which had hardly cleared by the time I reached the car park at Ashcott Corner. So I decided to make the best of the conditions by concentrating on bird *listening* rather than watching, which was indeed the only alternative for at least the next hour or so.

On the walk from the car park to the bridge over the canal – a distance of less than a mile – I counted 31 singing warblers of six species. Two of these I was hearing for the first time this year: the frenetic chattering of a Sedge Warbler, and the harsh rattle of a Whitethroat. As I peered through the mist at the latter bird, I noticed another small warbler a few feet below. Expecting to see another Whitethroat, I was surprised – and pleased – when my binoculars focused on a small, chestnut-brown bird with pale grey underparts: a Cetti's Warbler.

For of those 31 singing warblers, more than half belonged to this species. But it is one thing to *hear* Cetti's Warbler, and quite another to see it. This skulking little bird has by far the loudest song of any British songbird; a song so belligerent that the writer Simon Barnes created a mnemonic to remember it by: 'Me? Cetti? If you don't like it naff off!' (Only he used a stronger word . . .)

In fact the song of Cetti's Warbler is so memorable that once heard, it hardly needs a mnemonic by which to remember it. Yet paradoxically, this is a bird that hardly ever shows itself. So it was a rare and unexpected pleasure to spend thirty seconds watching this compact little warbler through my telescope, its long, rounded tail held cocked in the manner of a Wren.

As its foreign-sounding name suggests, Cetti's Warbler is a relative newcomer to our shores. It was named after Francesco Cetti, an 18th century Jesuit priest who made pioneering studies of the birds of Sardinia, his adoptive home.

Until the early 1970s, Cetti's Warbler was a major rarity in Britain, with only a handful of records. But since the early 20th century this skulking species had gradually extended its range northwards from its original home around the Mediterranean Sea. I can remember visiting Stodmarsh, in Kent, back in May 1975, primarily to see (or at least hear) this very species, which had just managed to hop across the Channel and colonise southern England.

What made Cetti's Warbler even more unusual was that at the time, unlike all our native warblers bar one (Dartford), it was a resident species, staying put all year round. Ironically this strategy almost led to its downfall, when two successive harsh winters during the mid-1980s killed off the nascent Kentish population. However, by then Cetti's Warbler had spread west to colonise Dorset and Devon, areas with a milder winter climate. As a result, the British population survived, and later spread back into east Kent.

Just as the sight of a Little Egret still brings a touch of Mediterranean exotica to our home turf, so the sound of a Cetti's Warbler, exploding out of the brambles alongside a Somerset reedbed, does much the same – at least for birders of mine and older generations.

It also brings a tingle of anticipation, making me wonder which new species might colonise Britain during the next couple of decades. Hoopoe, Bee-eater and Cattle Egret would be nice for starters . . .

Catcott Lows

Birding is rather like supporting your local non-league football team: you have to sit through mind-numbing hours of uneventful play before you hit on the ornithological equivalent of a nine-goal thriller.

Having had my fair share of nil-nil draws, I was being absurdly optimistic to think that an hour at Catcott would provide such excitement, but nevertheless, something told me this would be a good day. Perhaps it was the fine, warm weather; or the beautiful late afternoon light; or the fact that I was showing my friend and colleague Brett Westwood around my local patch for the first time.

Brett is the best naturalist I know – perhaps the best field naturalist in Britain. What he doesn't know about our native birds, mammals, flowers and insects could be written on the back of a rather small postcard. He can not only identify everything we see, but can also tell you all about the natural history of that particular species, some stories about its folklore, and often a well-chosen anecdote about when he last saw it. Unlike some highly knowledgeable naturalists, he is also great company, and always willing to share his knowledge with beginners – as he does regularly as a presenter on BBC Radio Four.

But today things didn't start very well. I opened the hide flaps fully expecting to find the male Garganey that I saw last Friday; but all I could see was the usual range of common ducks. A distant Yellow Wagtail improved things, but apart from a passing Kestrel and a couple of soaring Buzzards it was very quiet.

Then the atmosphere changed in an instant. The Lapwings' gentle calls turned into high-pitched cries of alarm, the ducks took to the air, and we had the unmistakable sight of a Peregrine powering towards us from the other side of the lagoon. Unfortunately, at that very moment a colleague chose to call me on my mobile phone, so as I juggled phone in one hand and binoculars in the other, my views of the falcon were less than perfect.

Peregrines are the fastest bird – indeed the fastest creature – on the planet; yet this particular individual was cruising as if out on a Sunday afternoon stroll. As he approached the hide, we could see every detail of his plumage: a dark, gunmetal-blue back; paler, mottled underparts; and the distinctive dark moustaches on either side of the face – all giving him the look of a bird not to be messed with.

In an instant, he turned, pulled his wings back and, from less than fifty feet above the water, shot down towards a hapless Lapwing. This time, the Lapwing escaped and the Peregrine flew off empty-clawed. Next time, I suspect, the target may not be so lucky.

A sighting like this brings a surge of adrenaline, and Brett and I were now alert to the possibility of anything appearing over the horizon. As I scanned with my telescope, I noticed another, larger raptor, soaring high to the east. It turned, and revealed the long wings, forked tail and brick-red plumage of a Red Kite – my first in Somerset.

By now we were on a roll. But the excitement of the kite was hardly over when Brett – using only a pair of binoculars – noticed another large raptor above the horizon. 'Surely that's not a Buzzard . . .' gave way to 'It's an Osprey!' A quick check with the scope revealed a large, pale bird of prey about the size of a Buzzard circling on broad, down-turned wings. Even at this distance, I could see the distinctive masked appearance that confirmed its identity as an Osprey. Flying Ospreys always look more like gulls than raptors, and I wonder how many passing birds go unnoticed, simply because birders are too lazy to look at every passing gull.

Time to go home, but not before a passing Sparrowhawk brought the total number of raptor species for the day – in fact the hour – to six. I thought back to my youth, when the sighting of *any* raptor – apart from the ubiquitous Kestrel – was a major event.

Days like these also make me recall the endless hours, days and weeks spent birding when nothing remarkable occurs, which made what we had just experienced all the more enjoyable. Definitely the birding equivalent of a 5–4 win in extra time!

FRIDAY 20 APRIL

Mill Batch

Although by nature an early riser, I still find it a lot harder to get up at, say, 4:45 as opposed to an hour or two later. But this morning I really didn't have much choice. It wasn't a work trip, or the children, that caused me to wake so early, but the opportunity to listen to the dawn chorus in my own garden, in the company of wildlife sound recordist Chris Watson.

To say that Chris is a good wildlife sound recordist is rather like saying Michelangelo can paint a bit, or that George Best was handy with a football. Chris is, without doubt, the very best in the world at recording the many and varied sounds of nature.

Chris is a tall, friendly man, whose native Sheffield accent has been overlaid with the tones of his adopted home, Tyneside. His naturally modest disposition conceals an extraordinary range of achievements, including being a member of the 1980s prog-rock band Cabaret Voltaire, a past that occasionally catches up with him. Not many people in our profession have two entries in the *Guardian*'s list of '1000 albums to listen to before you die', but Chris does.

Since leaving that world behind, Chris spent the next couple of decades developing his childhood passion for wildlife sound, which began when he used an eight-track recorder to capture the sounds of a Sheffield bird-table at the age of ten. Since then, he has worked with all the great wildlife TV presenters, including Simon King, Bill Oddie and Sir David Attenborough, and on many of the classic nature series.

Bill Oddie described him as 'the most intense and laid-back person I know', which nicely captures Chris's character; he is a regular visitor to our home, where he entertains both the children and us with his lugubrious sayings (example: 'I'm so hungry I could eat a buttered rat . . .')

Chris was in my garden to record birdsong for a Radio Four series on garden birds, in which I was appearing with Brett Westwood. And this calm spring morning was the perfect opportunity to do so; hence our early start.

As we walked down the lane beside the garden at five a.m., the first birds were already calling: distant Wood Pigeons, a few Rooks, and the first true songster – a male Blackbird broadcasting his song from one of the ash trees. Ten minutes later a whole chorus of Blackbirds and Robins – at least half a dozen of each – were belting out their songs at low pitch (Blackbird) and an octave or two higher (Robin).

Two swans flapping out of the rhyne (local word for watery ditch) at the end of the back field were complemented by a distant cockerel, which appeared to have had a lie-in; and the first cars, whose owners hadn't. Adding a touch of exotica was a peacock, which lives somewhere across the main road, and whose haunting, echoing cry seemed strangely appropriate for this very English dawn.

This was a chilly morning, made colder by the mist rapidly approaching across the fields, which soon obliterated our view of the Mendips and the radio mast over at Priddy. But the birds carried on regardless: Song Thrush, Wren, Blue and Great Tit adding their voices to the orchestra. Not until after half past five did the first summer visitor join in: a Chiffchaff, rapidly followed by a Blackcap. Why these migrants get up later than the residents I don't know, but it appears that they do.

Two larger birds, Collared Dove and Jackdaw, began at 5:45, but it wasn't until 6:15 – and sunrise – that the three finches, Goldfinch, Greenfinch and Chaffinch, finally joined in, along with a yaffling Green Woodpecker. The last to appear was the jolly little song of the Goldcrest, long after sunrise at gone half past six.

Chris popped in the house to warm up, while I totted up the total: 17 species, not counting domestics and exotics. But of course the dawn chorus experience is about far more than numbers. To the birds, it is the chance to win a mate, and the need to repel intruding, rival males who may take over their territory. To us, it has a far more pleasant feel to it: the joy and wonder of hearing something truly uplifting.

I'm always amazed at how few people have ever really heard a dawn chorus. It's not as if you need expert knowledge, or an exotic location; even if you live in the middle of a city there will, I guarantee you, be birds singing in the hour or so before dawn from March to May.

And for those members of my family who hadn't made such an early start, Chris kindly created a CD for us to listen to: a recording which reminds me of an unforgettable morning spent in the company of some wonderful birds, and a man who truly loves his work.

SATURDAY 21 APRIL

Mill Batch

The glorious weather continues; is April the new August? Were it not for the chilly mornings and evenings, it might almost be summer. The wildlife seems confused, too: a rap on the window from Suzanne while I was watching the football results informed me that the first dragonfly of the year had appeared in the front garden.

Sure enough, a female Hairy Dragonfly (if you look closely you can actually see the hairs around the thorax!) was perched on a lilac bush, giving excellent views.

Having spent most of my life ignoring any creature without feathers, I have been born again as a butterfly and dragonfly enthusiast, and have even invested in a net and some collecting boxes in order to study them more closely. Another sunny afternoon seemed a good time to try out my skills as a butterfly catcher, but after a few Bruce Grobbelaar-like attempts to dive into their path, I handed the net to my son James, to see if he could do any better.

He could. Despite having inherited his father's genetic inability to play sport, his seventeen-year-old reflexes were more than a match for our garden butterflies. Within an hour he caught eight specimens of six species, including a bedraggled Comma, dazzling Orange Tip and that tiny gem of spring days, a Holly Blue.

We transferred them from the net into a clear, plastic box and showed them to Charlie, George and Daisy, who were suitably enthralled – as, indeed, was I. Flight views of butterflies – like those of birds – never quite reveal their delicate markings; whereas a few minutes with a magnifying glass really do. A delightful afternoon, all the more so for the unexpected pleasure we got from such a simple pastime.

Once we had examined them, we released the butterflies, watching as they leapt forth into the blue sky like prisoners escaping from a maximum security prison – which, I suppose, is what it must have felt like for them.

Earlier this afternoon I received a phone call from a former colleague and old friend, Nigel Bean. Nigel and his family moved to Wedmore, just down the road, at about the same time as we relocated here; and ever since we have had a friendly rivalry regarding our respective 'garden lists'.

Up to now I have been winning – not least because our garden is a lot bigger, and with a better all-round view, than his – but today his skill and expertise began to tell. His voice could hardly contain his glee: 'Red Kite, soaring above the house. And . . .' – this is the important bit – 'it's heading your way!'

So while James leapt around the garden wielding his butterfly net,

I sat on top of the children's climbing frame (the highest point in the garden), watched, and waited. I did get two Buzzards, a dozen or so Swallows and a suntan; but, alas, no Red Kite.

In some ways this incident sums up the joys of garden birding. I may not have seen a kite today; I probably won't see one tomorrow. I may not even see one this year, or next, or the year after. But I can afford to take the long view. Given that I fully intend to stay here until I'm carried out in a wooden box, I shall surely see a Red Kite overhead one day. And, hopefully, lots of other great birds too.

SUNDAY 22 APRIL

Shapwick and Meare Heaths; and Mill Batch

A cool, fresh morning produced the first Cuckoo of the year – just as I was getting out of the car. I heard at least three more, but as usual didn't see one – though a female Sparrowhawk cruising low over the reeds gave me a momentary false alarm. On my way back to the car, I caught sight of a male Sparrowhawk perched on a pumping machine. For a few brief moments we looked at each other, his piercing yellow eyes staring intently – until he flew off and low, straight past me.

Later that afternoon, Nigel and Clare popped over from Wedmore with their children, Rachel and Thomas. Thomas is my only godson, and Nigel and I have vowed to make him a birder. Today seemed a bit early to start, as he is only 17 months old, so as the children settled down to play, Nigel and I took a stroll up to the end of our garden.

At first, we could hear only the usual species. But then we both heard a quiet, unassuming warble – a bit like a Blackcap warming up, but distinctive enough to make us both stop and listen.

It sang again, and this time the warble was followed by a rhythmic flourish of notes, rather like a distant – and not very tuneful –

Chaffinch. We both looked at each other and announced its identity in unison: Lesser Whitethroat.

Although tens of thousands of pairs of this tiny warbler breed in Britain, it must surely be a candidate for our least-known common breeding bird. Unlike its cousin the Whitethroat, which sits out on a bramble bush for all to see, and even launches itself into the air when it sings, Lesser Whitethroat is a skulking creature, which rarely emerges into the open.

And unlike the equally skulking Cetti's Warbler or Nightingale, it doesn't compensate for its retiring nature with a loud, distinctive song. So the challenge we faced was to get a decent – or even half-decent – view; which after much persistence, and having to fend off the attentions of various small children, we finally did. It's not all that much to look at really: a small greyish warbler with dark cheek-patches, but it was nice to confirm its identity.

[Postscript: Unfortunately this particular bird proved to be a passing migrant, and we didn't hear it again (but see August for details of an autumnal sighting).]

TUESDAY 24 APRIL

Mill Batch

'I've come to shoot your Rooks.'

The speaker is our neighbour, Rick, whose weather-beaten features and glint in his eye mark him out as a man who spends his life outdoors, and loves his work, despite its long hours and harsh nature. For Rick owns and farms many of the fields around us; indeed our home, Mill Batch, is the original farmhouse for his land.

We have enjoyed getting to know him and his family over the past few months, as like everyone else in the village they have been very kind and welcoming to us.

But this evening Rick had a shotgun cocked over his shoulder, and looked as if he meant business. 'I've just come to shoot your Rooks,' he said again, rather to my bemusement, adding 'if that's OK . . .'

Being a newly arrived townie, I didn't really feel I had much choice but to nod my assent. He is, after all, a sheep and cattle farmer, and presumably has good reason to dislike these ragged black birds. I made a rather lame joke about rook pie, and off he went. A few minutes later, I heard a rapid series of loud bangs, prompting a slightly tricky moment as I tried to explain to the children what was happening.

Next day, while wandering up the garden, I found a few glossy black corpses, and noticed that the rookery had fallen silent.

Apart from his antipathy towards Rooks, Rick is what conservationists call a wildlife-friendly farmer. His farmyard, to the side of our house, is regularly used to house his sheep and cattle, and as a result attracts insects which then attract birds – including our resident flock of House Sparrows I hear chirping in the hedge almost every day.

In spring and summer the farm buildings play host to nesting Swallows: those elegant visitors which grace the skies above our home from April to September, before they head south to spend our winter south of the Equator. Their place is taken by another elegant bird, the Pied Wagtail, several of which regularly perch on the tiled roofs, keeping their balance by moving their tail up and down.

SUNDAY 29 APRIL

Meare Heath

This spring I have seen more Garganeys than in the whole of the past decade. The first was at Catcott Lows in mid-April, since when I have enjoyed watching at least half a dozen, at various places around the Levels.

The best view came today at Meare Heath, a wetland reserve that is rapidly becoming my favourite local birding site. As I walked along the broad path, fringed on either side by reedbeds and shallow pools, I was again reminded of the marshlands of Eastern Europe – the unseasonably warm weather contributing to that illusion. Damselflies perched on lily-pads, Hobbies hawked for insects above my head, and the air was filled with the song of half a dozen different kinds of warbler.

Entering the hide, I sat down to enjoy the usual birds: a pair of Gadwall, some Tufted Ducks and a Moorhen with a solitary chick. Then I noticed a smaller duck swimming into view: a splendid drake Garganey. Despite his long and arduous journey to get here, his plumage was immaculate: a subtle combination of silvers, greys and browns, set off by the broad, creamy stripe across each side of his face.

The Garganey's curious name apparently originated in medieval Switzerland, and was first used in Britain during the 17th century. The species may have been commoner then, for it had already acquired a number of folk names, including one that is hardly ever heard today: 'cricket teal'.

I knew that this derived from its call, but even so I was taken aback when the Garganey I was watching suddenly uttered a low-pitched buzzing sound – very like that of a grasshopper or cricket, and not at all what you would expect from a duck.

He then proceeded to have a bath: moving gracefully from side to side to immerse himself in the water, then preening the long scapular feathers on his back with his bill. I could not have wished for a better view of this delightful little duck.

The Garganey is a rare breeding bird in Britain, with only a hundred or so pairs attempting to nest each year. According to David Ballance's *History of the Birds of Somerset*, a few do so in the Somerset Levels, though this does not usually become evident until the young are seen later in the season.

This particular male has not yet found a mate, but with luck he will. Perhaps, in a couple of month's time, I shall be treated to the sight of a pair with a brood of ducklings feeding on the pools at Meare Heath.

May

Two-year-old George is taking a particular interest in House Sparrows. Every time he goes in or out of our back door, their incessant chirping makes him look up and smile. From time to time, he stops to talk to them – and, as you might expect from a bird which has lived alongside human beings for longer than most, the sparrows talk back.

George's quiet, unassuming manner means he is occasionally over-looked in favour of his louder and more assertive siblings, so I think he finds a kindred spirit in these birds. Sparrows are so much part of our daily lives they have almost become one of us; and unlike more colourful, exotic or tuneful birds, we don't find much to celebrate in them.

At least that was true until recently. Sparrows were so common, so widespread, that we hardly gave them a second glance. Then some-thing very strange happened: they began to disappear from places where they had once been abundant. And paradoxically, as they vanished, so we began to realise that we hadn't appreciated them quite as much as we should.

As a child, I remember being taken to Regent's Park, and coming across the old man who fed the birds there. He would place some seed on his hand, and within a few seconds his open palm was covered with sparrows, eagerly accepting a free lunch. Then, he would pour the seed into our hands and let us share that incredible experience.

But a couple of decades later, when I returned to the park with a film crew and Bill Oddie, the sparrows had disappeared. They do still hang on in one corner of the park – in the cages of the animals at London Zoo – but from the rest of central London they have simply vanished. In Kensington Gardens, where Max Nicholson counted over 2500 sparrows in the 1920s, there are now none.

The reasons for the House Sparrow's rapid decline are complex. Indeed it is probably due to a combination of factors, including the lack of suitable nest spaces as eaves are boarded up and attics converted, a dearth of insect food for their young, and the disappearance of winter stubble fields where the birds used to feed.

So why, if they have declined so rapidly, do we have so many sparrows living with us here at Mill Batch? Because Rick's farmyard, right next door to the house, is still run traditionally – with regular movements of sheep and cattle, and as a result plenty of food for the birds. The hedgerows around the farmyard and our garden are a bit messy – the way sparrows like them – and the eaves of our house are full of spaces where they can wriggle underneath and nest.

As a result, the cheerful chirping of sparrows is a soundtrack to our daily lives; and George knows that whenever he hears it, he can look up and have a brief but mutually satisfying conversation.

Mill Batch

One of the greatest pleasures of living in the country is coming home from work on a fine, spring evening, and sitting out in the garden with a glass of beer, watching the children playing in the hay meadow . . .

This May Day, my idyllic reverie was broken by an unfamiliar sound – a series of piping notes, six or seven in all, coming from somewhere in the sky above. The first time I heard the call it barely registered; as a result of my relaxed mood I was not quite in full birding mode. The second time, though, I heard it loud and clear; and looking up, noticed a bird about the size of a medium-sized gull flying across the setting sun.

Grabbing the binoculars, I was just in time to register the long, pointed wings, mid-brown plumage, and the clinching identification feature: the decurved bill. That narrowed it down to two species – Curlew and Whimbrel – and to my delight the distinctive call confirmed its identity as the latter.

Amazingly, this bird has just travelled, in the last month or so, all the way from its winter quarters in sub-Saharan Africa. And its journey is far from over: it may be one of the few hundred that breed in the far north of Scotland, but it is more likely that it is heading much farther north than that. Like many species of wader that pass through Britain, the Whimbrel is a specialist of the boreal habitats that stretch around the globe, from Alaska and northern Canada, via Iceland and Scandinavia, to Siberia.

I have watched Whimbrels on Shetland, the one part of Britain that provides enough suitable habitat for them to breed in any number. I have also come across them in Africa: during our honeymoon in the Gambia, Suzanne and I regularly watched one feeding on the lawn outside our hotel room!

Mill Batch

For a few days, the fine, clear, dry and sunny weather has continued – the weather records revealing that April was the warmest in the UK since records began in 1914, and the warmest in England since 1657. Already, by the start of May, the back lawn has turned into a hay meadow – filled with yellow buttercups, docks, plantain and many other wild flowers I still can't put a name to.

I saw my first Swift over Meare village on the afternoon of 29 April, a few days after they had been reported in Bristol. But I had to wait until today, 5 May, to see one over the garden. In some ways the delay isn't surprising: we live in a rural area, and the most common summer visitors over our house are not House Martins or Swifts, but Swallows.

For the rest of the week, wet weather kept even these birds grounded, but after the rain finally stopped briefly a large flock of all three species came out to hunt for flying insects. Later in the month I heard a strange, grating call while on a family walk down the lane behind our house; it turned out to be a pair of Swifts mating in mid-air!

I love Swifts – in fact they are my all-time favourite bird. This choice may seem a bit strange, but consider the facts. If being a bird is about the incredible power of flight, then Swifts are, quite simply, the top bird. Their torpedo-like body and scythe-shaped wings allow them to sweep across our summer skies with consummate ease, screaming as they go – a sound that, combined with their dark colour, earned them the folk name 'devil-bird'.

Once they leave Britain, soon after fledging in July or early August, young Swifts fly all the way to Africa, then all the way back here the following spring. But because they are too young to breed, they fly around catching insects, before heading back south again. Finally, after another season hunting tiny insects under African skies, they return to us once again.

During all this time – about 21 months – they have not once landed anywhere, having fed and even slept on the wing. Only now do they seek out a building – a church tower or an old house – where they can breed.

The poet Ted Hughes summed up this miracle of nature – and its vital importance to us as human beings – when he wrote my favourite couplet in all bird poetry, in 'Season Songs':

They've made it again,
Which means the globe's still working . . .

I have a fear that one spring, around the start of May, I shall gaze up into blue, cloudless skies over the Somerset Levels, and see no Swifts. A week or two will pass, and they still won't be here. At that point – if it ever happens – we might as well shut up shop on Planet Earth, because we will have reached the point of no return.

Earlier today, I took our old friends Phil and Frances down to Shapwick and Meare Heaths for an afternoon walk, on what would turn out to be the very last warm day of May. Not surprisingly, dragonflies and damselflies were out in force, with my first Banded Demoiselles of the spring, and dozens of the bulky Four-spotted Chaser, the insect equivalent of one of those First World War bi-planes.

There were a few birds, too: most interestingly single Whimbrel and Spotted Redshank – both migrants on their way from Africa to the Arctic – on the drained pool. What was most striking to me, though, was the difference between what I was doing, and Phil and Frances's agenda for the outing.

I suppose I shouldn't be surprised if some people don't have the same obsessive interest in the natural world as I do. My companions were delighted simply to be out in the English countryside on a beautiful spring day – to take a pleasant walk. But for me, the day was full of tension and promise – would a migrating Osprey fly over, for example? (It didn't.)

Berrow Beach

George and I snatched a swift half-hour down on the beach. While he ran up and down, bending over to pull up great clumps of wet sand in his hands, I swiftly scanned the tideline for signs of life. There were a dozen or so Oystercatchers, resplendent in their pied plumage with that huge, orange bill (looking like someone has stuck a carrot onto their face), and a single Whimbrel feeding along the tideline.

Out to sea, half a dozen Kittiwakes were heading west with the larger gulls, while swallows and a few terns – probably Arctic, but too far away to tell – were flying east.

But the most interesting birds were on the surface of the sea itself. As the wind blew the waters up and down, I caught an occasional glimpse of five large, dark ducks. Even from this distance, I knew that they were Common Scoter – no other duck has quite the same black solidity. In fact the name 'scoter' is, famously, a misprint: it was originally 'sooter' – a reference to the bird's dark plumage – but was transcribed wrongly at some point in the distant past, and the new name stuck!

Common Scoters are not so common on this coast, and this was a good sighting. They were probably heading back to Scotland to breed on some windswept loch in the Flow Country.

I have always been interested in bird names and their origins; the fact that I chose to do a degree in English rather than Zoology, despite my passion for birds, probably explains why.

Checking out that reference for the scoter, I leafed through a slim volume, now long out of print: *The Oxford Book of British Bird Names*. Written by a former Professor of Germanic and Indo-European Philology at the University of Reading, W.B. Lockwood, you might expect it to be a rather dry read, but in fact it retains a fine balance between scholarship and entertainment.

As well as 'proper' names, the author also relates the origin of obsolete names such as 'goatsucker' for the Nightjar; and a selection of folk names, ranging from the familiar 'yaffle' for the Green Woodpecker to the delightful 'coal-and-candle-light' for the Long-tailed Duck.

I'm not always entirely convinced by the author's contentions: he claims, for example, that 'Lapwing' is a corruption of an Anglo-Saxon phrase meaning 'movable crest', and that 'Fieldfare' actually means 'grey piglet'. But the book is one that I continually refer to, either to check the meaning of a name or simply to browse, as this entry shows:

Fallow Chat. A name for the Wheatear, found locally from Surrey to Somerset, and also recorded from Scotland (Banff). The bird commonly frequents fallow land, while onomatopoeic CHAT occurs again in STONECHAT, originally a Wheatear name.

This kind of detailed scholarship – based on a lifetime's work, yet covering a subject of obvious interest – seems to me to be in decline nowadays, probably because while publishers only want bestsellers, academics focus on even more narrow fields of study.

June

Shapwick and Meare Heaths

The dragonfly never knew what hit it. Its nemesis approached, quite literally, out of the blue: at first with wings swept back, to gain speed. Then, as the predator neared the unwary insect, it braked suddenly, bringing its legs forward and body back. Claws gripped tight, and in one smooth movement the dragonfly was lifted up towards its mouth, dispatched and eaten.

The predator was one of a dozen or so Hobbies, our most elegant – and arguably most delightful – falcon. I watched as the birds gorged themselves on a harvest of flying insects while soaring effortlessly in the sky above the reserve. Having returned from Africa in late April, up to fifty Hobbies gather here during May and early June, before dispersing to breed across southern England. In the meantime they provide their human spectators with our annual entertainment.

When I was growing up, the Hobby had an almost mythical quality. They were said to breed somewhere on Salisbury Plain, with perhaps a few pairs in the New Forest. The entire British population numbered fewer than a hundred pairs, and because of the perennial threat from egg collectors their nesting locations were kept a closely guarded secret.

I can still remember the first Hobby I ever saw, back in the spring of 1975. We were at Westbere, in Kent's Stour Valley, when what looked like a giant Swift shot past us. I had never seen a bird looking so sleek and streamlined.

As well as the shape, it was the plumage details that caught my eye: the dark hood contrasting with white cheeks, slate-blue back, streaked underparts, and that deep orange patch at the base of the tail. Having spent years gazing at Kestrels and trying to turn them into Hobbies, the sight of the genuine article was a revelation. My love affair with the species began that day.

Since then I have seen dozens – perhaps hundreds – of these splendid birds. Nevertheless, watching them hunting so expertly over my local patch has still been one of this spring's highlights.

This bird has a curious namesake: I recall, at the age of nine or ten, being given a table football set by the older son of a neighbour across the road. I was always puzzled by the name, 'Subbuteo', and even more so when a few years later I discovered that the scientific name of the Hobby is *Falco subbuteo*. I assumed this was a coincidence, until in the mid-1990s I read the obituary of the game's inventor, Peter Adolph.

It turns out that when he tried to register the name of his invention, just after the Second World War, he wanted to call it 'The Hobby'. But having been prevented from doing so, he did the next best thing, calling it 'Subbuteo' (a Latin compound meaning 'small buzzard'). Since then several generations of children have enjoyed playing the game, presumably unaware of the ornithological origins of its name.

*

The Hobby is also one of those birds that have the power to turn the heads of novice birders. On a fine Saturday afternoon in early June, I took a work colleague, his two sons and two of their schoolmates out for a taste of birding. The Hobbies were almost the first bird we saw, and even a bunch of pre-teenage boys were impressed. As, indeed, was I.

Jeremy is keen to introduce his sons and their friends to the pleasures of wildlife watching; and Shapwick on a sunny day seemed a good place to start. The two older boys Sam and Tom (aged 11 and 12), turned out to have excellent eyesight and observational skills, and while their younger brothers Ted and Josh (both aged nine) were less engaged than their siblings, they still showed that curiosity typical of youngsters when faced with something new and different.

The Hobbies' status as ace predators clearly made an impression, and the boys were also keen on the Cormorants we watched from the Noah's Lake hide. The allure of these weird, rather prehistoric looking birds was enhanced by the way they perched in a row of dead trees that emerge from the water like dead men's limbs.

But I was really impressed when, as we left the hide, Tom noticed a small, rather unobtrusive insect. Having heard me name it earlier, he confidently identified it as a Blue-tailed Damselfly – showing just how quickly children can learn. I only hope that this trip has sparked some enthusiasm in him, and that he continues to pursue his new-found interest in birds and other wildlife.

SUNDAY 17 JUNE

Collard Hill, Somerset

Father's Day, and I am allowed to decide how we are going to spend the morning. I glance out of the window, where sunshine is struggling to break through a layer of cloud, and tentatively suggest a family walk.

Actually, that's not quite true. I tentatively suggest a family walk to see Britain's rarest butterfly, the Large Blue. A colony of these delightful insects lives on a hillside near the town of Street – about half an hour's drive away.

To my surprise and gratitude this is accepted; and even the children seem excited about the prospect. I suppose if you want to capture their imagination, suggesting we go in search of a 'large, blue butterfly' is pretty well guaranteed to work. I just hope they aren't too disappointed when it turns out to be about an inch long, rather than the giant insect they may well be imagining.

We were accompanied on our excursion by two dear friends, Nigel and Cheryle Redman. Nigel is almost as obsessed with butterflies as I am. Cheryle is not obsessed with butterflies at all: poised and elegant, she would rather spend her Sunday morning at the garden centre. Or shopping. Or in bed. Or indeed almost anywhere but walking down a steep, grassy slope accompanied by three children, in search of a blue butterfly.

We managed to get out of the house soon after 11 a.m. (virtually an all-time record), arrived at the site, and parked in the youth hostel car park. The novelty of a short walk through a wood (we live in a treeless zone on the Somerset Levels), and a travellers' camp (I had forgotten that Glastonbury starts next weekend), was followed by a death-defying dash across a busy road to the reserve itself.

A brief word about the Large Blue. Despite its rarity, this is a story of success rather than failure. Large Blues went extinct in Britain in 1979 – due, it seems, to conservationists' obsession with removing domestic livestock from nature reserves.

It turned out, after the event, that sheep were crucial to the lifecycle of this splendid butterfly: by keeping the grass short they allowed a certain species of red ant, on which the Large Blue depends to raise its young, to thrive. No sheep meant no red ants – and, therefore, no Large Blues.

So the ones we had come to see have been given a helping hand – reintroduced, as the jargon puts it – by dedicated conservationists. The scheme has been such a success that not only have the sites been made public, but this particular location, Collard Hill, has retained open access.

So today we weren't alone. Indeed, far from it. At least a couple of dozen butterfly twitchers, for want of a better phrase, were straggled out along the path, eyes gazed downwards. The short grass of this flower-rich meadow is ideal for butterflies, and there were plenty to see.

Marbled Whites, one of our most striking insects, flitted across the grass in good numbers, their dappled skewbald pattern apparent even at a distance. They were joined by the ubiquitous Meadow Browns and the less common, but equally dull-looking, Small Heaths. A Painted Lady, my first of the year, was a good sighting. But where were the blues . . .?

Our quest received an added frisson from two things: first, the fact that we were accompanied by three small children with attention spans the length of a very short piece of string; second, the potential presence of the Common Blue butterfly, which as its name suggests is quite common, and is also remarkably similar to the Large Blue. Indeed the only ways to tell them apart are the dark (not orange) spots on the underwing of the latter, and the dark spots on the upperwing. Technical stuff – and not all that easy to see on a breezy day.

Then we saw it – or at least we saw a blue butterfly. Tantalisingly, it whipped along a few inches above the surface of the hill, constantly threatening to land, but never quite doing so. Nigel and I were 99% certain it was the species we had come to see – but, as with birding, you need to be 100% sure before you can count it.

As we walked back up the slope to where Suzanne and Cheryle were waiting patiently with the trio of children, we hit the jackpot. A surprisingly diminutive blue butterfly flitted weakly over the wild flowers, then landed and began to feed. I approached to within a few metres and checked with the binoculars – and things were looking good. To make certain, Charlie and I approached so close that I needed my reading glasses to check out the markings. Not a sign of orange anywhere on the underwing – Large Blue in the bag.

Charlie seemed to sense my excitement and the fact that this beautiful insect really was something special. We crouched down to nose level and simply marvelled at its delicate features. I tentatively advanced a hand; and the butterfly crawled onto my fingertip, paused briefly, then flew off. A truly magical moment – all the more so for being shared with friends and family. Even Cheryle was impressed, though I still think she and Suzanne would have preferred a morning at the garden centre.

FRIDAY 22 JUNE

Mill Batch

With the Glastonbury Music Festival set for this weekend, and Wimbledon starting on Monday, it's hardly surprising the weather is so awful. The tabloids' new phrase for this midsummer gloom is 'Monsoon in June', so I wasn't surprised when yet another morning dawned cloudy and muggy, after overnight rain.

Up and about before the rest of the family, I popped out the back door to take some laundry out of the washing machine in our outhouse. On my way back I heard what, in my sleepy state, I took to be an unusually chatty sparrow.

A few moments later, as I sat down in my study to log on to the computer, I heard it again, just outside my window. The penny finally dropped – it was a Reed Warbler, in full song! I rushed outside, to be regaled by that unmistakeable, repetitive sound – not from a reedbed, but from the heart of a lilac bush.

After a spot of pishing I managed to get good but brief views of the bird: the typical unstreaked plumage and rufous-brown colour confirming its identity. But what on earth was it doing here?!

Three theories:

(i) It was a local bird which, for reasons best known to itself, had decided that reedbeds are monotonous and wanted a change of scenery. Unlikely.

(ii) It was a young bird recently fledged from the nest. Yet it looked like an adult to me; and besides, do young Reed Warblers sing? Very unlikely.

(iii) It was a migrant, from the north of Britain or even farther afield, that had been passing overhead – for like most songbirds, Reed Warblers travel by night – when it got caught in the wet weather and decided to take shelter where it could. Plausible, and much more interesting than theories (i) and (ii).

Whatever the reason, it certainly provided me with a memorable moment. When I returned from work that evening there was neither sight nor sound of it – reinforcing the migrant theory. But if that's the case, it means that just one day after the summer solstice, autumn has begun!

SATURDAY 23 JUNE

Burnham-on-Sea

A family walk before tea, 'to blow away the cobwebs', as Suzanne describes it. Without binoculars, I am forced to enjoy the birds *'au naturel'*. Lots of 'seagulls'; a single juvenile Black-headed Gull loafing on the beach; but best of all, a baby Starling along the prom. The children find him hilarious, and chase after him. Having fended them off,

I notice how young he is: just out of the nest and barely able to fly. His chances of survival? Pretty low, I suspect . . .

The next morning another baby bird causes excitement in the Moss household. One of George's sparrows has somehow got inside the house. After some effort, I catch him, and we release him outside. Again, I wouldn't rate his chances very highly.

As some unromantic (but realistic) scientist once pointed out, if every single baby bird survived to breed the following year, after a few years we would be knee-deep in them . . .

THURSDAY 28 JUNE

Mark

I was suffering from the after-effects of a nasty virus, but on my last day off work felt well enough to take the children down to the local playground for some fresh air. As we arrived in the car park, I noticed a movement out of the corner of my eye. Three or four House Martins were collecting mud from the smallest and most temporary of puddles.

In the air House Martins have a characteristic compact appearance. On the ground a very different shape revealed itself: as they momentarily touched down they appeared strikingly blue above and white below, with shaggy 'trousers' of feathering down each leg. They swiftly picked up beakfuls of mud, and then flew off to the nearby houses to add another tiny piece to their nest, before returning for some more.

House Martins are rapidly declining, partly because we are a bit too tidy nowadays – too quick to fill in holes in the ground where they might find some building material.

The last time I saw them doing this was about seven years ago, on a new housing estate in Chippenham where bulldozers had left craters which had then filled with water, providing the perfect consistency of mud. I bet those puddles have long gone, and the local martins have to travel much farther to find their nest material.

Watching these birds, I was reminded of Bill Oddie's memorable comparison between the appearance of House Martins and that of Killer Whales – next time you see a House Martin close-up, check out that pattern of black and white for yourself, and you'll see what I mean!

FRIDAY 29 JUNE

BBC Canteen, Bristol

Whenever I can, I have lunch with my friend and colleague Brett Westwood in the BBC canteen. As I have already mentioned, Brett is the finest all-round naturalist I know – able to identify and tell you fascinating things about any plant or animal he comes across, from beetles to birds, sedges to hoverflies and much more besides.

But Brett has a rather shameful secret: every now and then, he and his mates get up at the crack of dawn and drive hundreds of miles, all to see a particular rare bird. Yes, they are twitchers.

If pressed on the subject, Brett affects a lack of interest, almost a disdain, for this pastime. Like someone who has given up drinking or smoking, he will admit to 'the occasional one', but when pressed harder, will confess to a series of lapses.

This particular lunchtime he was weighing up alternative ways of spending his weekend. The first: a detailed survey of the wildlife of Wyre Forest, near his home in the Midlands. The second: a full-blown dash up the motorway to the Scottish Borders, to see Britain's fifth White-tailed Plover.

Now, White-tailed Plover is undoubtedly a lovely bird – I know, because I once saw one in Israel. But is it worth spending a weekend to see – or worse still, wasting a weekend failing to see?

For me, the answer is simple. Even if the bird were thirty miles away rather than three hundred, it would take a lot to persuade me to go to see it. If it were just down the road at my local patch, I probably would – but that doesn't count as twitching because I would be going there anyway. I am like the reformed drug addict, who genuinely doesn't need his fix anymore, and can gloat rather smugly at those who do.

In the end, Brett made the right call: he stayed at home looking at shield bugs and micro-moths; his friends went, and they 'dipped' – the bird had flown. However, when the plover turned up at Leighton Moss in Lancashire the following weekend, Brett did go, and successfully twitched it.

But as he reminded me on his return, 'the trouble with twitching is that the best you can do is *not* fail!' He had seen the bird, and quite enjoyed it, but there was still a faint hint of dissatisfaction in his voice.

All this reminded me of when I used to be a twitcher. Not a full-blown one – and certainly not the type who would drive overnight from London to Scotland, or charter planes from Scilly to Wales, or lie awake in agonies if I dipped on a bird.

I was more of a part-time, weekend twitcher. If I was free and heard about a rare bird in Sussex or Kent, I would happily drive a couple of hours each way to try to see it. Sometimes I did; often I didn't. If I still had a good day's birding despite missing out on the big prize, I was generally content.

But I was well and truly cured of the twitching bug one day in May 1993. The weekend before, I had successfully twitched one of Britain's first Oriental Pratincoles (an impossibly exotic Asian species) in Norfolk. So when, on the Saturday night, my friend Neil called to see if I wanted to go up to Norfolk again so that he could see the bird, I told him I had other fish to fry. I would spend my precious free Sunday in Kent, twitching two species of warbler I had yet to see in Britain, Sardinian and Great Reed.

A word of explanation: both these species are common around the Mediterranean, and I had seen them both very well – abroad. But in those days my 'British List' was paramount, so I needed to see them on home turf for them to count. Absurd, I know – but those are the rules.

First, I endured a two-hour, ninety-mile drive to Dungeness. Then, a fruitless and frustrating tramp around the shingle with a crowd of fellow twitchers, each hoping for a glimpse of Sardinian Warbler, one of the most skulking of all its family. But the weather was far too windy, and the bird sensibly stayed hidden. So after a couple of hours, I gave up, cut my losses, and headed north to the RSPB reserve at Elmley on the Isle of Sheppey.

Arriving at Elmley, I walked along the track to where the Great Reed Warbler had last been seen. Almost the size of a thrush, this bird is like a Reed Warbler on steroids, with a song to match. Even as I approached, the body language of a small crowd of disconsolate-looking twitchers made me realise the bird was not there. A silent reedbed confirmed its absence. Two down, none to go.

Then, as I sat vainly hoping the bird would miraculously appear, a message came up on a fellow-birder's pager. He looked incredulous. 'Pacific Swift at Cley, in North Norfolk'. I thought of Neil, down the road at the pratincole, and wondered if he had also heard the news. I must admit I felt a twinge of envy and frustration – envy that he would probably see this, one of the ultimate rarities ever to appear in Britain, and frustration that I had wasted my day on a wild warbler chase when I could have been with him in Norfolk.

I drove home disconsolately. That evening Neil called with good and bad news. Bad – despite waiting several hours, he hadn't seen the pratincole. Good – he got the last car parking space in Cley and had cracking views of the Pacific Swift. Then, as the icing on the cake, he saw a Desert Warbler along Blakeney Point. Both were major rarities; both would also have been new sightings for me.

Yet strangely, Neil also felt a sense of failure, for *not* having seen the bird he had originally gone for, the Oriental Pratincole. While not feeling much sympathy for him, I could see his point.

Soon afterwards, I gave up twitching. OK, I would still go to see a rare bird in my local area; even divert a few miles if it was something I had never seen anywhere in the world, like the Ivory Gull in Suffolk in December 1999 (see *This Birding Life*).

But like someone free from a former addiction, I had become an ex-twitcher – and am all the happier for it. Twitching can be fun; it can be exhilarating, exciting and a great way to meet fellow birders. But it can also be deeply frustrating and unsatisfying. For me, seeing a Lesser Whitethroat in my garden, or watching Hobbies hunting over my local nature reserve, is so much more satisfying than any storm-driven rarity can ever be.

SATURDAY 30 JUNE

Westbury-sub-Mendip, Somerset

Birders are friendly sorts, by and large; usually willing to swap information to help a fellow birder see something good. So when, a few weeks ago, I received an e-mail out of the blue asking about sightings of Red Kites in Somerset (still a local rarity), I was happy to respond.

A couple of weeks later, Sue, my cyber-correspondent, sent me another e-mail – only his time she wasn't asking my advice, but offering a sighting of her own. One of our most delightful summer visitors, a pair of Spotted Flycatchers, was breeding in her garden.

Spotted Flycatcher chicks are only in the nest for a couple of weeks, so time was of the essence, despite the poor weather. By the time I arrived with my old friend Graham Coster (Charlie's godfather and the publisher of this book), the four well-grown young were almost hanging out of the open-fronted nestbox, only a day or two away from fledging.

It was hard to believe that the flycatchers had chosen this particular spot. Sue's garden is actually a terrace built on top of her garage, and though packed with flowers and greenery, is still pretty small. But these birds, which had flown all the way from West Africa to this little corner of Somerset, seemed perfectly at home.

We waited in her hallway, staring through a rain-spattered window for a few minutes. Then, with a rapid movement, the flycatcher was there. Perching momentarily on the fence, it flew to the nestbox, deposited a beakful of flies for the chicks, and dashed off.

The process repeated itself again and again, and gradually we began to understand the pattern behind the bird's movements. Its mate joined in too, so we were treated to really fabulous views of these increasingly scarce little birds.

The Spotted Flycatcher has suffered a catastrophic decline in the past couple of decades. Once a widespread and locally common summer visitor, it is now very thinly spread – and it is always a privilege to see one. As with so many of our declining songbirds, we don't quite know the reasons behind this drop in numbers, though a reduction in flying insects at home, and drought on its wintering grounds in West Africa, are the most likely causes.

Superficially this is another 'little brown job', but on a close view its delicately-marked plumage – plain brown back, wing-feathers with pale fringes, the little collar of spots on the upper breast, and a delicately streaked cap – mark it out. The head shape is especially pleasing: the streaked cap giving the appearance of a slight crest; the beady black eye; and the unusually flattened, broad bill just perfect for catching flies.

It is here that the Spotted Flycatcher really comes into its own. Sallying forth from a perch, it will grab a fly in mid-air, its long wings giving it absolute control and enabling it to manoeuvre itself into just the right position to snatch the unfortunate insect.

After a while, we set up Sue's telescope to observe the wooden fence where the bird kept landing, and were rewarded with exceptional, frame-filling views. I could even see the tiny notches in the feathers around the eye. All in all, it was a real privilege – made all the more enjoyable by meeting a fellow birder with such enthusiasm. And if the weather ever clears up, Sue has promised to take me on a Nightjar hunt before the season is over.

As Graham and I were about to drive off, I noticed what I took to be a brightly-coloured butterfly in the next-door garden. Something about its fluttering movement made me realise it wasn't anything familiar – and a look through the bins confirmed this. I could see a flash of scarlet and black, while closer examination revealed a striking pattern of white and yellow spots on the upperwings.

As another joined it, we called Sue, who came out bearing a moth field guide. The black and white pattern on the forewings, together with the bright scarlet hindwings, and day-flying habits, all pointed to one species: the aptly named Scarlet Tiger. Skinner, author of the moth guide, says that the species 'flies freely in sunshine'. What they were doing in the pouring rain is a mystery.

LATE ON SATURDAY 30 JUNE

Mark, Somerset: That blasted albatross . . .

Also during the course of this weekend, an extraordinary series of events has been played out on the SOS website – and in the emotions of birders throughout the county and beyond. Here's a blow-by-blow account of what has been happening:

FRIDAY P.M.

A man glances out of his window at Brean, just up the coast from Burnham-on-Sea, and notices a strange bird in his front garden, looking like a huge seagull. When it fails to fly off he telephones the local wildlife rescue centre, who come along to pick up the bird and take it back to their HQ, so they can check it out for illness or injury. One of the centre volunteers tentatively identifies the bird as an albatross – and assumes that it is the species which normally occurs in British waters (albeit still only occasionally), a Black-browed Albatross.

The name of the centre, Secret World, turns out to be ironically appropriate, as the owners, either not realising the importance of their find (or perhaps realising all to well), decide to keep the news to themselves.

SATURDAY A.M.

After a night in care, the albatross appears fit and well. Meanwhile the Secret World staff have tried to contact a local birder, leaving a message on his answer phone. But he is in Scotland and only gets the message on his return – too late for the events that followed.

Meanwhile, Somerset's birders – including me – remain blissfully unaware that this incredible bird is in our midst.

SATURDAY P.M.

The albatross is taken to the top of Brean Down, a huge rocky outcrop sticking out into the Bristol Channel, where it is released. It flies off strongly out to sea, and finally out of view. The release is photographed, and also filmed using a hand-held video camera.

When Graham and I return from our birding on the Saturday afternoon, I casually log onto the SOS Messageboard. What I see first intrigues, then amazes me, and finally leaves me in paroxysms of frustration.

Local birder James Packer has posted a link to the official Burnham-on-Sea website, which tells the whole story of the albatross being discovered, taken into care and released. James bemoans the fact that the news hasn't reached local birders in time for anyone to see it, and suggests that we continue to look out for the bird off various coastal watchpoints.

Then, an hour or so later, James posts some truly astonishing news. He has tracked down some photographs of the bird in question; as soon as he looked at them, alarm bells began to ring. The bird's dark head and the pale yellow line along the top of the bill leave him in no doubt: this is no ordinary Black-browed, but the much rarer Yellow-nosed Albatross.

To put this into perspective: Black-browed may be rare, but birds do sometimes turn up in British waters, and even spend time in Gannet colonies where birders have a chance of seeing them. But the Yellow-nosed Albatross has only been seen once before in Europe, and never in Britain. This is the twitchers' Holy Grail – a British first – and it has eluded our grasp.

I must confess to mixed feelings at this point. I like to think that I am no longer interested in chasing up and down the country after rare birds – and indeed that is the case. But this bird was on my local patch – and what a bird! It is not just its rarity that makes it so extraordinary, but the sheer unlikelihood of its appearance. And, as the photographs showed, a real beauty. I have been stomping around the house, cursing my bad luck.

Later this evening, footage of the albatross's release has even appeared on YouTube, rubbing salt into our wounds. It shows the albatross at the moment of release, as it was transformed from a gangling, clumsy creature – flopping about in the arms of its rescuer – to a bird of great beauty and elegance as it took to the wing.

For many local birders, this is just too much. Incensed at having been unable to twitch the bird, they are now venting their frustration on the SOS website. Toys have been thrown out of prams: first by the angry twitchers, lobbing insults at the bird's rescuers; then by those defending the actions of Secret World.

I can see both points of view – and also I wonder why the bird's rescuers hadn't realised that they were sitting on an ornithological goldmine. If they had released the news in time to attract a large crowd of twitchers they could have raised a substantial sum in donations to support their fine work.

As a colleague of mine has just noted in his e-mail: 'Anything that frustrates twitchers' god-given right to see a bird can't be all bad!' And ironically, purists amongst the twitching fraternity couldn't have counted it anyway, as, having been taken into care, the bird had become invalid for listing purposes . . .

Myself? Ultimately I'm torn between amusement at the twitchers' reaction, and a latent sense of frustration. Whether or not you can 'count' a bird like this seemed to me beside the point. I would just love to have seen it, for the once-in-a-lifetime experience of watching this majestic wanderer from the southern hemisphere on my local patch. But for me, and the rest of the Somerset birders, it will forever be 'the one that got away'.

July

Edford Woods, Somerset

After the emotional ups and downs of the previous day, a disappointing outing to a new location: a wooded part of east Somerset very different from the watery flatlands around my home. I was accompanied by local birders John Hansford and Graham Turner. John is a frequent contributor to the SOS website, regaling us with sightings of the wide range of woodland birds to be found near his home, while Graham had travelled a few miles south from Bath. Charlie's godfather Graham Coster came along too.

The four of us had a pleasant walk through the woods, enjoying good company and fine conversation. So why was it so disappointing? The usual reason birding trips fail: bad timing. We had come too late in the year, when most birds have stopped singing, making them much harder to find. And we had chosen one of the wettest days of a very wet summer, the dampness and cool breeze giving a distinctly autumnal feel.

This combination of weather and season meant that hoped-for songbirds failed to appear, sensibly hunkering down in the woods. Our best sightings were a couple of Bullfinches and a Roe Deer – and the first blackberries of the autumn.

Still, sometimes birding turns into a social event, and is no less enjoyable for that. And I do plan a visit back here later in the year, as John's efforts on his local patch have produced some really good sightings . . .

SATURDAY 7 JULY

Shapwick Heath

In middle age, I find myself increasingly drawn to groups of wildlife other than birds. Like many birders before me, I have developed a fascination with butterflies, dragonflies and damselflies. These are the ideal groups for a novice to get to grips with: highly visible, delightful to watch and relatively easy to identify.

So when I saw that Natural England was running a guided butterfly walk at Shapwick I was keen to go along. The day dawned breezy but bright: not ideal, certainly, but not disastrous either.

A group of us met at the Peat Moors Visitor Centre in the heart of the Levels, and once leader John Burrell had rounded us all up, we set off on our quest. John is one of those quietly authoritative local experts, men of a certain vintage (now mostly over 50) who learnt their natural history the proper way, out in the field, with no shortcuts to earning their expertise. From the start we knew we were in for a revelatory experience; now all we needed was for the butterflies to show up.

And show up they did. The first grassy patch produced both Large and Small Skippers, small, moth-like butterflies which hold their wings in a characteristic folded pose when settled. Meadow Browns, Ringlets, and single Small Tortoiseshell and Gatekeeper continued this promising start, along with the usual Large and Small Whites. John's keen eyes also spotted two Great Green Bush-crickets, one of our largest and most magnificent insects, beautifully camouflaged as they posed on stems of grass.

We had been warned that the recent heavy rain had left the woodland trail very boggy indeed, so stepped carefully as we followed the path. We had three target species – two of which, Purple Hairstreak and White Admiral, would be 'lifers' for me. These two woodland butterflies could hardly be more contrasting in appearance and habits. The Purple Hairstreak likes to perch on oak leaves, often high in the canopy, its small size and camouflaged appearance making it very hard to spot; while the White Admiral is a large, showy, black-and-white insect with a strong and direct flight.

Yet it was the Purple Hairstreak which we saw first, and which turned out to be abundant in this short stretch of woodland ride. Eventually we got views down to a few inches, revealing the deep purple upperwings and delicately marked underwings.

Soon afterwards, John picked out the first of two White Admirals. Like its familiar cousin the Red Admiral, this is a strikingly attractive creature: its dark upperwings bisected by broad white lines. Again, we got excellent views.

I had seen our third target species, Silver-washed Fritillary, before, but never tire of watching this beautiful insect. Rich orange in colour, and patterned with black streaks and spots, it gets its name from the pale silver wash on its underwings. Males often chase the females along sunlit rides, with a persistence that usually pays off as they are finally allowed to mate.

The wood also yielded commoner butterflies: Green-veined White, Brimstone, Red Admiral, Comma and Speckled Wood; along with newly emerged Peacocks, looking splendid in their bright colours, and a couple of Holly Blues. All in all we tallied 18 species, an extraordinary total given the limitations of time, weather and habitat – and on my return home I added a 19th, the first Marbled White I have seen in our garden.

I am now well and truly hooked, and for the remaining couple of months of summer I intend to seek out more of our local butterflies. Perhaps it's the brevity of the season that appeals, or the aesthetic beauty of my quarry. Or maybe it's just the novelty of getting to know a new group of creatures, reminding me of what birding was like when I was a child, and everything was exciting and new.

The fine weather continued into the afternoon, giving me my first chance for a few weeks to mow the back lawn. This is rather like painting the Forth Bridge – a seemingly endless chore during the spring and summer months.

However, it does provide me with the ideal opportunity to spend time in the garden and hopefully notice a few birds. Today was a good example. While cutting the lawn I flushed a small brown finch – almost certainly a Linnet, which unfortunately flew off before I could get much on it.

Fortunately, half an hour or so later, it came back. Despite being unable to grab my bins in time because I was carrying a cuppa and a chocolate biscuit, I did manage to identify the bird as our first Linnet for the garden – a long-awaited arrival given that they breed just half a mile behind our house, down Perry Lane.

SUNDAY 8 JULY

Mill Batch

Early next morning I took a stroll around the garden with my mother-in-law, June. The Linnet (or another one) was still there, together with a baby Robin, newly out of the nest, perched on the garden bench in a classic pose.

As we strolled down the path, we could hear a bevy of Blackbirds uttering that familiar scolding call. Senses alerted, I scanned the apple trees, only to see a shaggy, chestnut-brown bird fly out of the first tree and off into next door's garden. Its rounded wings and clumsy flight marked it immediately as a Tawny Owl – no wonder the Blackbirds were so upset.

WEDNESDAY 11 JULY

Mark; Shapwick and Meare Heaths

A short cycle ride with Suzanne along the lanes at the back of our house produced some surprises: several Linnets along the hedgerows, together with plenty of singing Skylarks. Both are classic farmland species in decline, so it's good to see them here. Maybe farming has finally turned the corner, though a few more properly managed arable fields would help attract the seed-eating species.

That evening I popped down to Shapwick on a twilight quest – and a successful one too. Just before dusk, I sat in Noah's Lake Hide as a pale, ghostly bird emerged from its hiding place in a battered tin shed in the middle of the reedbed: a Barn Owl.

To an evening chorus of Reed Warblers he floated past the hide, giving brief but excellent views. A few minutes later a juvenile bird appeared at the window of the hut. After almost a year in Somerset I was beginning to wonder if I would ever see a Barn Owl – now I've broken my duck I shall probably find dozens of them!

Berrow Beach

Birding before breakfast is always satisfying, all the more so when the birds deliver the goods. In my former life in the London suburbs I was more than an hour's drive from the coast, so an early start was essential. Here in Somerset things are rather more leisurely: so although my alarm didn't go off until seven, I still managed to get to the car park at Berrow beach by quarter to eight.

I took a short walk across the golf course, accompanied by an obliging Sedge Warbler singing his heart out from a hawthorn bush, to reach the beach. Timing is everything along this coast: at low tide you can barely see the sea, let alone any birds. But my timing was perfect, with the water barely 50 metres beyond the line of sand dunes at the top of the beach.

At first, it seemed fairly birdless, apart from the usual flock of Black-headed Gulls, each 'foot-paddling' to disturb tiny marine creatures along the tideline. Farther along the beach I glimpsed a more promising sight: a tightly bunched flock of Oystercatcher, at their high tide roost. Alongside them, there were nine Curlews and a single Black-tailed Godwit in breeding plumage.

But what I had really come to see was seabirds. The odd albatross aside, Bridgwater Bay is hardly renowned as a seawatching spot. Nevertheless, persistent westerlies blowing up the Bristol Channel have brought a number of seabird sightings off this coast.

So as I walked along the beach I alternated between scanning the shoreline and looking out to sea. As often happens with seawatching, I was almost ready to call it a day when a sub-adult Gannet flew straight into my binocular view, only a short distance offshore. As it came past it banked from side to side, revealing the extensive black mottling along the rear of the wings that showed it to be a three-year-old bird.

Like buses, when one seabird comes along you usually get another, and today was no exception. First a dozen or so birds in the distance, alternately flashing black and white as they twisted and turned on stiff wings, barely a foot or two above the waves: a flock of Manx Shearwaters. Then the Gannet flew back the way it had come.

Just as I was leaving, buoyed by the thought of a fried breakfast, something made me glance back at the shoreline. A gull flew past, and the bright white wings immediately made me realise it was something interesting. As it turned, revealing an all-black head, it confirmed its identity: a beautiful adult Mediterranean Gull in full breeding plumage. The bird landed offshore, foot-paddled for a moment or two, and then started to swim.

In the past two or three decades Mediterranean Gulls have gradually extended their range northwards from continental Europe, and now regularly breed at various gull colonies in southern Britain. Yet another example of how the ranges of birds can change – sometimes, as in this case, within a single lifetime.

SUNDAY 15 JULY

Mill Batch

St Swithun's Day dawns predictably wet and cloudy. As the 'make-or-break' day in British weather folklore, it seems appropriate that this particular date sees the first signs of autumn in the garden: at dusk, little flocks of Starlings heading south-east, towards Westhay, together with groups of Black-headed Gulls flying off to their roost at Cheddar Reservoir.

FRIDAY 27 JULY

Mill Batch

A cloudy and humid evening produced at least ten Swifts, with a few Swallows, overhead, heading purposefully south-west – are these the first migrants leaving us? Last year's Swifts had gone by the final week of July – will there be any here this August? In the meantime, the weather has continued dull and wet – the weathermen say it's the wettest June and July on record, with major floods only about 50 miles north of here, in Gloucestershire.

Friends and relatives phone to check that we are OK. Fortunately, not only is our house about 15 metres above sea level, at the highest point in the village, but this landscape has been designed over centuries to deal with flood water.

The first settlers in Somerset were known as the 'summer people', after their practice of farming these low-lying lands in summer only. Sensibly, they made sure to build their homes and villages on the few areas of slightly higher ground. They also dug hundreds – perhaps thousands – of dykes, ditches and drains, known locally as rhynes, which soak up any excess water and largely prevent the area from flooding.

TUESDAY 31 JULY

Near Priddy, Somerset

Of all our breeding birds, perhaps the most mysterious is the Nightjar. The poet John Clare wrote a wonderfully evocative (and characteristically punctuation-free) account of the bird he called the 'Fern Owl':

They make an odd noise in the evening beginning at dew fall and continuing it at intervals all night . . . one cannot pass over a wild

heath in a summer evening without being stopt to listen & admire
its novel and pleasing noise it is a trembling sort of crooing sound
which may be nearly imitated by a making a crooing noise & at the
same time patting a finger before the mouth to break the sound like
stopping a hole in the German flute . . .

The very first time I saw a Nightjar was back in the summer of 1984.
I was on a whistle-stop tour of East Anglia, trying to catch up with several species missing from my British List.

It was about five o'clock in the afternoon, and I was walking across
Westleton Heath, not far from the RSPB reserve at Minsmere, when I
heard a very peculiar sound. The *Collins Bird Guide* describes it thus:

A far-carrying, hard reel, at close range amazingly rattling and
intense, which, with only brief pauses, carries on 'in two gears' for
hours on end, 'errrrrrrrrrurrrrrrrrrerrrrrrrrrurrrrrrrr . . .' from dusk to
dawn.

Well, it certainly wasn't dusk, but that was the perfect description of
the sound I was hearing. I walked towards where it seemed to be
coming from – a gorse bush protruding from the surrounding
heather – when to my amazement a bird floated up into the air just a
few feet in front of me, still uttering this extraordinary sound.

I noted the bark-like plumage; bulbous, whiskered head; and the
white flashes near the tips of the wings, before the apparition flew off.
It was one of the most memorable first sightings I have had of any
British bird.

This summer, consistently wet and windy since early June, hasn't
been very suitable for looking for Nightjars. So it was that on the
very last day of July – almost the end of the Nightjar season – a
party of four of us set out to a site on the Mendips to search for
the bird. I can't tell you exactly where, as unfortunately Nightjars

are still scarce enough as a breeding bird to be the target of egg collectors.

As we arrived, the weather conditions looked promising: cool, but calm, with a clear sky. Not surprisingly, we weren't alone: as we arrived at the right place – an open area of heathland within a spruce plantation – my companion Sue spotted a fellow birder.

It turned out to be Keith Vinicombe – one of the best-known birders not just in this part of the country, but nationally. Keith regularly writes forensically accurate identification articles for *Birdwatch* magazine, a publication to which I also contribute. Yet strangely, we have never met. As often happens when I encounter one of Britain's top birders, I was struck by his quiet, modest manner – real experts don't need to shout about their knowledge and abilities, I usually find.

In a Livingstone-Stanley type of greeting, we solemnly shook hands and settled down to wait. But not for long. Within a minute or two we heard the classic 'churring' noise, and a few seconds later the bird was momentarily aloft in the evening sky.

I always forget what a distinctive, uniquely jerky flight action Nightjars have: they seem to bounce through the air on long, extended wings with their body and tail suspended below. On this male bird we could easily see the prominent white wing-patches used in display, as well as smaller white markings on the sides of the tail.

During the following twenty minutes or so, we were treated to a series of brief but satisfying views, including one bird perched on top of a spruce, and another resting on the sandy path ahead of us. In an unforgettable moment, we also witnessed the rise of a stunning harvest moon, glowing deep orange in the rapidly fading light.

Satisfied from both the ornithological and aesthetic viewpoints, we walked back to the car. On the way home we enjoyed an unexpected bonus, as Sue treated us to a close-up view of a glow-worm in the hand: a deeply unnatural pinprick of intense, lime-green light emanating from the rear end of a rather modest-looking little bug.

But as I fell asleep that night, the experience uppermost in my mind was the sound of a churring Nightjar, and the final lines from Clare's sonnet on the bird:

> . . . teazing round
> That lonely spot she wakes her jarring noise
> To the unheeding waste till mottled morn
> Fills the red east with daylights coming sounds . . .

August

Mill Batch

The chattering hordes of Swallows in the blue sky overhead signalled a welcome improvement in the weather, so once again I took advantage of the unexpected sunshine to cut the lawns around our house. Even so, this is hardly the long hot summer of last year, and the sight of ripening apples and blackberries reminded me that autumn is now only just around the corner.

By mid-afternoon, as I emptied the grass box for the umpteenth time, I noticed a sudden change in tone to the Swallows' sounds. As I looked up, a taut, swift-like figure could only mean one thing: a Hobby, on the hunt for a meal.

The atmosphere was palpably tense – as if all sound had stopped, apart from the loud urgency of the Swallows, frantically calling to their newly fledged young.

With a flick of its wings, the Hobby dived: a streak of slate grey against the deep blue. It disappeared behind the trees, and I held my breath; would it rise with a Swallow in its talons?

But the Swallows had sounded the alarm just in time, and were safe – for the moment at least. A few minutes later the same thing happened again, only this time the Hobby was joined by a second bird – hunting in a pair.

Later on, the Swallows flew high in the sky, uttering their usual cheerful sounds – their brush with death apparently forgotten.

THURSDAY 9 AUGUST

Mill Batch

While I enjoy the challenges of butterflies and dragonflies, whose relatively small number of species makes them manageable for a beginner like me, moths are another matter. Even if you exclude the 1500 or so 'micro-moths', we are still left with over 800 different species to consider.

Time to get in an expert: preferably one with his own moth trap. So it was that on one of the few fine evenings this summer, my friend and fellow writer Dominic Couzens arrived at dusk with the 'proper' equipment.

Dominic will be familiar to most wildlife enthusiasts as the author of several excellent books on garden birds, and a regular contributor to *BBC Wildlife* magazine. He and I get on very well considering the differences in our characters: Dominic's quiet, deliberate way of observing and understanding nature is light years away from my more gung-ho approach; and I admire him for that. And of course we share a passion for British wildlife, so I always look forward to spending an evening with him.

After a convivial supper we set the trap. After a quick rearrangement of egg-boxes (more about that later) and a connection to an extension lead, the light was on. Within seconds, moths began to flit around us – and with the seasoned experience of a veteran mother (that's 'moth-er' rather than mum) Dominic began to give them names.

And what names! Burnished Brass, Setaceous Hebrew Character, Flame Shoulder, Buff Ermine, and the longest of any British moth, the Lesser Broad-banded Yellow Underwing (not, of course, to be confused with the Lesser Yellow Underwing, plenty of which were also present).

My head exploding, I tried to commit their shape, colour and character to memory. Not easy in the dark, but with persistence I began to make sense of some of the different species. Brimstone was easy, as like the butterfly of the same name it is a buttery yellow. Yellow Tail was easy because it was the only pure white moth present. Rosy Footman, a delicate pink in hue; and Buff Footman, wearing its wings like a long footman's cloak. And a stunning Leopard Moth – pale with black spots.

Next morning, we dragged Charlie out of bed at 7 a.m. and he – and we – watched in amazement as we saw the moths in daylight for the first time. The function of the egg boxes finally became clear: they serve as a hiding place for the moths as dawn breaks into their nocturnal world.

Charlie proved rather quicker at identifying the moths than me – and enjoyed seeing them crawl over his hand. My – and his – favourite is the Buff Tip, a moth which when at rest looks exactly like a section of birch twig, newly cut with a penknife. Only when you touch it, and it moves, do you realise that it is a living creature.

I am now well and truly hooked, and studying the field guide to moths (concise version) avidly. Who knows, I might become a 'moth-er' myself.

As we were setting the moth trap we heard a peculiar, single-note call coming from low overhead; swiftly followed by another. Dominic, who knows his bird calls a lot better than me, looked baffled for a moment – then gave his verdict. He wasn't 100% sure, but he thought it may have been a Coot.

If that sounds unlikely, bear in mind that every autumn more than four thousand Coots gather at Cheddar Reservoir, a few miles to the north – and no-one ever sees them come or go. Being weak fliers, and therefore very vulnerable to aerial attack, we assume that Coots migrate by night – so the chances are this may be what we heard. Another 'one that got away' . . .

SUNDAY 12 AUGUST

Ham Wall, Shapwick and Meare Heaths

Another Sunday afternoon, and in a change from the usual weather pattern this summer, a rather fine and sunny one. I snatched a couple of hours down at my favourite haunts, Shapwick and Meare Heaths; only this time I walked in the opposite direction from the car park, towards Glastonbury.

This took me onto the RSPB's reserve at Ham Wall, which is really an extension of the Natural England reserve at Shapwick, making this one of the largest continuous areas of reedbed in southern England.

It was a quiet day for birds, as I would expect in the middle of August, so I turned my attention to another group of flying creatures – dragonflies and damselflies.

I am ashamed to say that until about six or seven years ago I took virtually no interest in 'dragons and damsels', these airborne beauties of the spring and summer. In fact I can pinpoint exactly where and when my fascination with them began: on a filming trip to Wicken Fen, for the second series of *Bill Oddie Goes Wild*, in July 2001.

Wicken Fen is by far the smallest place we have ever attempted to film a half-hour programme – but it worked. The reserve, owned by the National Trust, has the distinction of being the oldest in Britain, having been originally bought by the Trust in 1899. Long before, in the 1820s, a young Charles Darwin collected beetles there; and it still boasts one of the finest selections of plants and animals in East Anglia, perhaps in the whole of Britain.

Of all the creatures found there, one of the main attractions is the range of dragonflies and damselflies. During the course of a few days' filming – in suitably fine weather – we saw about 15 species. Given that there are only about 35 different kinds in the whole country, seeing almost half of them in one place was bound to get me interested – and it did.

With the help of ebullient dragonfly expert Ruary Mackenzie Dodds, a larger than life character who runs the National Dragonfly Museum nearby, I learned a few facts about dragonflies: that they spend up to seven years underwater as larvae, before emerging for just a few weeks in their adult form; that they evolved millions of years ago, and would have flown with the dinosaurs; and that the best time to look for them is on a warm, sunny day, at pub opening time.

I was also reminded that there are two basic kinds of 'dragonfly': the true dragonflies, whose wings are held out at right angles from the body like those of an aeroplane; and the smaller damselflies, whose wings are held along the body when closed.

I discovered the differences between the sub-groups of dragonflies: hawkers, chasers, darters and skimmers, each of which – just like birds – has their own particular and distinctive 'jizz'. With a bit of practice, I soon became adept at picking out the more distinctive species: the massive, blue Emperor; the small, neat Common Darter; and the Brown Hawker, whose wings are a delicate yellowish-buff, visible even at a distance.

But the species I found most fascinating was one of the largest damselflies: the wonderfully named Banded Demoiselle. This is the medium-sized insect you often see in good numbers in June or July, as they emerge from their larval state and fly for the very first time. I could hardly believe that I had never noticed it before – but then the same is true of the other 'dragons and damsels'.

Now that I am tuned into them I have finally realised what it must be like to have no interest in birds. Presumably you simply don't notice them, while I – and all the other birders out there – am constantly aware of their presence.

Today, at Ham Wall and Shapwick, I saw six different kinds of dragons and damsels, a respectable if unspectacular total. Most damselflies are spring creatures, but there were still plenty of Blue-tailed and Red-eyed Damselflies to be seen – the latter showing their crimson bug eyes when I looked closely at them through binoculars.

There were also Emperors and Southern Hawkers cruising up and down the rhyne; Black-tailed Skimmers sunbathing on the path; and plenty of Common Darters, some of which were rather brown, which my spotter's guide tells me makes them 'mature'. That would mean several *months* old rather than several years, for the adult dragonfly's life truly is, in Hobbes's famous phrase, 'solitary, poor, nasty, brutish and short'.

After an hour or so, I repaired to the Railway Inn for a refreshing pint. The Railway won't win awards for the best gastropub in Somerset – in fact all you can usually get to eat is a packet of crisps – but it is a good, honest local with decent beer and a friendly welcome. I sat outside, enjoying an unfamiliar sensation – that of the sun shining on my face – a rare event in this dreadful summer!

FRIDAY 17 – SUNDAY 19 AUGUST

British Birdwatching Fair, Rutland

Funny, isn't it, how when you are a child, each year takes what seems like aeons to pass, whereas when you reach my age they flash by rather too rapidly for my liking. For well over a decade, the Birdfair has been one of the highlights of my year; though it does seem to come round rather too quickly nowadays.

The Birdfair (or British Birdwatching Fair, to give its full title) began as a little local event during the late 1980s. By the time I first visited, in the early 1990s, it was already the highlight of the British birding calendar; and soon afterwards it went global, with birders and wildlife enthusiasts from every part of the world converging on England's smallest county on the third weekend of August each year.

This time, the weather forecast promised heavy rain on the Saturday and Sunday, and so the Friday was the busiest ever. I arrived mid-morning (having failed to get my act together to come down the night before), and had to park in a rather distant field. But a swift walk brought me to the entrance, and once again I launched myself into the fray – what fellow birder Tony Marr once memorably described as 'three days of interrupted conversations'.

For the joy of the Birdfair is that everyone in the birding world seems to be here – not just British birders, but friends from Trinidad & Tobago and the Gambia, California and New Jersey, Australia and Israel: almost every corner of Planet Birding.

You start talking to someone, and within seconds your eye is caught by someone else. It's rude to interrupt your first conversation, but if you don't, it may be another year before you see the other person again. I am sure there are people who have met once at the Birdfair, ten or fifteen years ago, and never quite managed to speak to one another since!

How different from the first time I came here, back in 1992, with my friend Neil, his daughter Amy and my son David. The two five year-olds were in their element, but Neil and I found it all a bit overwhelming.

The following year I went again, this time helping on the *Birdwatch* stand, as I had just begun to write for the magazine. The next couple of Birdfairs were amongst the most enjoyable: I was just getting established as a writer on birds, and getting to know more and more people each time I went. My *Birdwatch* colleagues, led by editor Dominic Mitchell, were great company, and gradually I came to realise that some of the world's top birders were also amongst the most modest and delightful people you could ever hope to meet.

In 1995, my book *Birds and Weather* was published, and I enjoyed the unfamiliar sensation of being recognised by strangers for the first time. I can still remember a man sidling up to me carrying a copy of the book, which he had just bought from the bookstall next door. 'Bloke there says you'll sign this . . .' he stated, thrusting it into my hand. Slightly surprised that anyone should want my autograph (apart from on a cheque), I duly signed. I hope he's still got his copy – the print run was so small they are now selling on the internet for over £100!

In 1996, I brought a film crew here to make an episode of the very first series of *Birding with Bill Oddie*. Back then, Bill hadn't quite attained the cult status he has today, and could wander around more or less unmolested. Today, when he visits the Birdfair, he gets mobbed by eager autograph hunters, who obviously realise that his signature is worth more than mine.

The resulting film gave, I think, a pretty good picture of the Birdfair back in those days, before it 'growed and growed' into the behemoth it has become today. There was a kind of innocence then, summed up in the traditional one hour 'mini bird race' we captured on video for posterity. Today, sadly, there doesn't seem to be time for such pastimes – the need to network, and of course to do business, has seen to that.

Not that I'm cynical about the Birdfair. It continues to do a great job: raising the profile of birding, and raising a small fortune for conservation projects in the developing world. And it's still great fun – if you haven't been, do try to attend.

Until last year, Suzanne had been to every Birdfair since we first met back in 1997. Two years ago, she even brought all three children – who at the time were aged just 21 months, six months and six months respectively. I can still remember Charlie wandering up on stage during one of my presentations, to the amusement of all present – apart, of course, from me.

This year she planned to bring them again, but unfortunately the weather was so bad that she called off the trip. So I wandered around the sodden marquees on my own, stopping to chat to my dear friends Sheila and Marleen from Cape May Bird Observatory in New Jersey, who kindly invited us to their autumn birding weekend next October. This time we really will try to go, as it's been far too long – more than seven years – since we were last there.

One of my favourite times at the Birdfair is the Saturday afternoon, when if the weather is good we sit outside the catering marquee in a loose assembly of friends and acquaintances, have a beer or two, and catch up with people's news. This year it was far too damp and cold to do that, but I did have an encounter which sums up the nature of the Birdfair.

I was passing the stand of Birding Poland, and my friend Marek Borkowski and his wife Hania invited me in for refreshments. We first met in the late 1990s, when we visited Poland with Bill Oddie and made one of our most memorable films there. I shall never forget Bill and Marek climbing on the top of his ancient Russian ex-army truck to get a better view of Aquatic Warblers, one of Europe's rarest and most elusive birds.

Back to this year. I sat and chatted with Lasse Laine, one of the top Finnish birders, a delightful, big bear of a man. Out of the corner of my eye, I saw a dark-haired man with a beard approach the stand, have a brief conversation with Marek, and start to walk away. I called him back, and introduced him to my two companions.

It was Josep del Hoyo, once a country doctor from Catalonia, who back in the 1980s embarked on the most ambitious bird publishing project ever attempted. *Handbook of the Birds of the World* has now reached its 12th volume (out of 16) and is widely regarded as the greatest series of bird books ever published.

HBW, as it is known, has changed Josep's life. Today he travels the globe, seeking out new information about the world's birds and their habitats – and doing as much as he can to help save them. Strangely, two countries he has yet to visit are Poland and Finland.

So I stood back as these three men – each the acknowledged expert in their field – discussed possible future projects, which will hopefully involve Josep visiting their home countries. Only here, in a muddy field in England's smallest county, could a Catalan, a Pole and a Finn be conversing in English. What has brought them together, of course, is their mutual love of birds.

TUESDAY 21 AUGUST

Mill Batch

In search of a sledgehammer in order to put up a clothes line in our back garden, I popped across the road to our neighbour Mick, who works miracles in his allotment here despite a constant battle with the prevailing westerly wind. Mick knows his birds, so when he told me that he has regularly seen a Little Owl in the field next door, I abandoned my errand and rushed home for my binoculars.

Sure enough, as I scanned the hedgerow in the late afternoon sunshine, I found a pair of bright yellow eyes staring back at me. The owl sat, enjoying the sunshine, halfway up an elder ripe with dark, succulent berries.

This was my first sighting of a Little Owl since we moved down here over a year ago, and all the better for being (just) viewable from my front garden, enabling me to count it on my rapidly growing garden list.

Little Owls are so much part of the English countryside it's easy to forget that they were only introduced to Britain from the continent just over a century ago. Unlike most other non-native species they don't seem to do any harm, and have been accepted by birders and non-birders alike as a welcome addition to our avifauna.

The next morning I heard a familiar honking – but not a sound I've heard over this particular garden before. It was a flock of almost 40 Canada Geese – another introduced species, but one nowhere near as welcome as the owl.

These two species brought my garden list – species seen in, over and from, my garden – to 68. I am now level with my friend and colleague Brett Westwood, though as he has pointed out, he lives in a Victorian semi in the middle of Stourbridge, so doesn't have the advantages of location and aspect that I do. He also mentioned, in passing, that his previous garden at Cookley in North Worcestershire had a list of 101, including Alpine Swift, Osprey, Ring Ouzel, Storm Petrel, Kittiwake and Quail! I am suitably crushed.

My rivalry with Dominic Couzens is a little more even-handed. He has the advantage of having five years' head start on me, and of living by a heath in Dorset, which means that Dartford Warbler is a regular sighting. On the other hand I am a bit nearer the coast, and have a much larger area to watch over and from. He is currently on 83 species, so I am hard on his heels. However, now that a year or so has gone by, new additions have become much harder to acquire, and I shall need to put in many more hours if I have any hope of catching him up!

Meanwhile my friend Nigel Bean, down the road in Wedmore, has gone for quality rather than quantity: as well as the Red Kite I mentioned back in April, he saw a further two Red Kites and the much rarer Black Kite over his garden in the space of a week.

FRIDAY 24 AUGUST

Middleton Lakes RSPB Reserve, Warwickshire

Birding has long been considered rather a middle-class pastime, which anyone with any real experience will tell you is very far from the truth. But it is fair to say that whole sections of British society rarely, if ever, venture onto a bird reserve. Young families, especially from inner cities, and members of Britain's Black and Asian communities are noticeable by their absence.

Fortunately, the RSPB has started to address this in the most practical way possible: by creating reserves in or near major cities, with easy access for millions of people. Back in March I travelled to Saltholme, on Teesside, the new flagship reserve for the north of England. Today I visited one a bit nearer home: Middleton Lakes, near Tamworth in Warwickshire.

Just three miles from the busy M42 Birmingham ring road, these disused gravel quarries are being turned into what has just been designated the RSPB's 202nd reserve. Its accessibility – less than an hour's drive from all the major cities in the Midlands, and only a couple of hours from London and the north-west – means that it is forecast to attract at least 40,000 visitors a year by the time it opens to the public in 2009.

A stroll around with site manager Nick Martin opened my eyes to the possibilities of the place. A pair of Spotted Flycatchers hawked for flies, while a Willow Tit – another rapidly declining species – chattered noisily in the scrub alongside the canal. And it wasn't just birds: Purple Hairstreak and Small Copper butterflies, and a whole host of dragonflies and damselflies, were taking advantage of one of this summer's rare sunny days.

Nick is under no illusions as to the huge task facing him and his colleagues; but he is also fired by the possibilities of creating a place which can reach out beyond the traditional, middle-class membership of the

RSPB to attract young, urban families and other city dwellers who haven't previously visited any kind of nature reserve.

If they succeed, it will be an appropriate place to do so. For at the entrance to the reserve is Middleton Hall, dating back to the 14th century, and currently being restored to its original state.

In an oak-panelled room, Professor Ian Dillamore of the Middleton Hall Trust gave me a potted history lesson. I learned that during the late 18th century, the hall was the home of Francis Willughby and John Ray, two men who between them virtually invented modern natural history.

After Willughby died unexpectedly in 1672, his friend and protégé Ray published the first bird book written entirely in English. *The Ornithology of Francis Willughby of Middleton in the County of Warwick* marks the point at which natural history turned from being superstition and guesswork into a modern scientific discipline based on accurate observation.

John Ray went on to revolutionise the world of botany, laying the foundations for the classification system we still use today. Largely neglected in comparison to his more famous contemporaries such as Isaac Newton, he has been described by his biographer C.E. Raven as 'the English Aristotle, with whom the adventure of modern science begins'.

I like to think that during a break from his studies he might have wandered the fields alongside the River Tame near Middleton Hall, and enjoyed the abundant birdlife of this hidden corner of the Midlands countryside.

And that more than three centuries later, he would approve of the work being done here: work to create a place where people from all walks of life can come for a day out and enjoy Britain's greatest free natural resource – our native wildlife.

Mill Batch

A truly autumnal feel to the morning, which dawns foggy, with Robins singing their plaintive autumn song, a family of Goldfinches feeding on the thistles, and a couple of Swallows perched on the wires in the farmyard. There have been lots of House Martins and Swallows here recently, feeding themselves up with insects in preparation for the long journey south. I shall miss them when they go.

A patch of wild mint has come into bloom on the sunny side of our garden, surrounded by fluffy thistle-heads and the stunningly beautiful (though of course non-native) yellow evening primrose flowers.

The mint has proved a major attraction for butterflies, and today, amongst the commoner Small Tortoiseshells and Gatekeepers, I noticed two smaller, less frequent visitors. The first, a tiny, exquisite creature with coppery-orange upperwings spotted with black, was the aptly-named Small Copper. Its cousin, the Large Copper, is now sadly extinct as a British species, though plans are underway to reintroduce it to East Anglia. The smaller version is good enough for me: a jewel-like creature unobtrusively feeding on the purple flowers of the mint.

Then I saw another tiny butterfly. The Common Blue is less common than its name might suggest, so I caught it in my net to confirm its identity. After showing it to the children, I released it back onto the mint to stock up on nectar.

A colleague recently told me that at the turn of the 20th century there were no fewer than 25,000 butterfly collectors in Britain. Nowadays we no longer collect and kill them, yet our butterfly populations are in freefall because of the widespread overuse of pesticides and the loss of habitat. The Victorian collectors have been much criticised, but as well as teaching us much of what we now know, they also respected their quarry. I'm sure Darwin would have been horrified to discover how few butterflies now flit across a typical stretch of the English countryside . . .

Mill Batch

Taking down the washing from the line after breakfast, I noticed a movement at the top of our elder bush. It was a Lesser Whitethroat, in newly-minted juvenile plumage, scoffing elderberries as if its life depended on it.

Which in a way it does. For this tiny bird, about the size of a Great Tit, will in a week or so undertake a truly epic migratory journey. Like other summer visitors, Lesser Whitethroats travel each autumn to Africa, but they take a rather unusual route. Instead of flying directly south, they head all the way across Europe and the Middle East to Turkey and Israel, before taking a sharp right turn, crossing the Red Sea to Ethiopia. Some European birds then continue westwards as far as Niger.

A glance at a world map reveals this to be a bizarre route, especially for those birds breeding in Western Europe such as the one in my elder bush. But it gives an important clue as to the evolutionary history of the species. Like many in the same genus, known to birders as '*Sylvia* warblers', the Lesser Whitethroat's ancestral home is in south-east Europe, south-west Asia and the Middle East. Gradually, over many generations, their range extended north and west, finally reaching Britain.

But these birds retained their ancient migration patterns, embedded deep in their DNA. So although we can see that it would be quicker to cross the Mediterranean at Gibraltar in the west, for them the more circuitous journey makes perfect sense.

For me, watching a Lesser Whitethroat out in the open is always a real treat. Back in the 1990s I remember seeing them in the Red Sea port of Eilat, where migrating birds – some possibly from Britain – feed in the local park. But at home I've only ever seen them diving into hedgerows or dense bushes, never to reappear.

The sighting was even more memorable as I got the chance to use the new eyepiece on my telescope. Magnified at 32 times normal size, this tiny bird filled the frame, allowing me to see every single detail of its feather patterns. Eventually it got bored of me watching, or had eaten its fill, or both, and flitted away.

That evening I cycled a few miles along the back lanes to the Wheatsheaf pub at Chapel Allerton with my teenage son James. As we rode along, I caught sight of a large, dark raptor flying low over the fields, being mobbed by crows.

Instantly I knew I was looking at something different from the local Buzzards. In the moment of panic as I ground to a halt, leapt off my bike and fumbled for my binoculars, both Red and Black Kite went through my mind.

In fact it turned out to be something a bit less unusual, but still great to see: a female Marsh Harrier, with a deep chocolate-brown plumage set off by a creamy crown.

Harassed by the crows, the harrier dived for cover and didn't appear again. Brief, but memorable.

Oddly, despite being so common now in East Anglia, Marsh Harriers are quite a rare sight here on the Somerset Levels, at least at this time of year. Later on, in autumn and winter, there are usually two or three birds hanging around the Avalon Marshes, but this is the first I've heard of recently. It was probably a passage bird, heading south – perhaps all the way to Africa.

The first time I ever saw Marsh Harriers was at Minsmere in 1973. What is truly remarkable is that, at the time, the male and two females I saw from the Island Mere Hide were supposed to be the only breeding birds in the whole of the country (Marsh Harriers are generally polygynous, with the male taking several females).

Marsh Harriers are one of bird conservation's greatest modern success stories, and a particular credit to the RSPB. In the thirty years or so since my first encounter with them, they have not only increased in numbers but also spread north and west. There are rumours of them breeding somewhere on the Levels, and they probably do, but understandably such events are kept quiet for fear of attracting the tiny but persistent band of egg collectors still practising their black arts.

WEDNESDAY 29 AUGUST

Mill Batch

Just before dusk, I wandered over the road to Mick's allotment to see if I could spot the Little Owl, which I heard calling the other night. To my surprise, Mick was still here, and beckoned me over. 'You're a bird man; maybe you can tell me what these are.'

Flushed with pride at being called a 'bird man' by a proper countryman, I peered at the photos he had taken. They showed two slightly blurred views of the same species: a pale, upright songbird with a dark eyestripe, wings and tail. His book told him they were Tawny Pipits, but he knew that this species is a major rarity here. I could see what he meant, but having fetched my glasses I could confidently identify them as Wheatears; migrants from northern Britain, or possibly Scandinavia.

There are, apparently, several of them on the hay bales a few fields away. I made a mental note to pop along there tomorrow.

Mick also showed me a truly extraordinary picture: of at least 40 (probably more) Grey Herons in a single field, taken last winter on nearby Tealham Moor. According to Mick this is an annual event, but only lasts a day or two. 'I suppose they're pairing up,' he suggested. He is probably right – but it's something I've never seen this usually solitary bird doing.

THURSDAY 30 AUGUST

Berrow Beach and Blackford Moor

I made another early start, to catch the high tide at Berrow before the dog walkers come along and spoil it for the birds – and birders! As I emerged from behind the dunes I caught sight of a tight little flock of about 150 Sanderlings running along the tideline.

I inched forward, crouching, so as not to frighten the birds, and was rewarded with intimate views of these beautiful little waders. It's often said that Sanderlings look like little clockwork toys – and they do – but they also have a sleekness and elegance which marks them out from the more run-of-the-mill Dunlin.

At this time of year they are mostly moulting out of their orangey breeding garb and into their pale, frost-grey winter plumage. Their feathers need to be in tip-top condition, for these truly are amongst the greatest global travellers of the bird world.

In late summer, they leave their breeding grounds high in the Arctic and head south – along the coasts of North and South America, Europe, Africa and Asia – even as far as Australasia. Almost any sandy beach in the world may, at some time or other, play host to a flock of these delightful waders.

Including, to my delight, this little beach at Berrow, just a few miles from my home. What a privilege it is to be a birder, and to spend a few minutes watching these birds as they refuel before heading off south once again. Before long, a large Irish Wolfhound crashed over the dunes and down onto the beach; the Sanderling scattered to the winds, and the magic moment was over.

Before I returned home for breakfast I took a brief diversion to the moor a mile or so behind our house. As Mick said, a field full of hay bales also contained two Wheatears, each perched upright on a convenient stack.

And to my surprise and delight, along the nearby rhyne were half a dozen slightly smaller, more upright birds, each sporting a distinctive pale eyestripe and orangey breast: Whinchats. Both these species are migrants, stopping off on their journey south. And both go almost as far as the Sanderling: the Wheatears (probably from the north of England) and the Whinchats (from nearby Salisbury Plain) winter way to the south of the Sahara desert.

I got into trouble with Suzanne for saying so, but autumn is most definitely here!

FRIDAY 31 AUGUST

Tadham and Tealham Moors

For the past year, whenever I have returned home at night I have diverted along the narrow road that runs across Tealham and Tadham Moors. The reason? I am convinced that one night I shall see a Barn Owl, ghost-like in the headlights.

Finally, tonight was the night. After a long and exhausting drive from Peterborough via Devizes, I turned down the lane without much hope of success. But within a couple of hundred yards I caught sight of a distinctive shape on a post to the side of the road. Sure enough, it was a Barn Owl, glowing pale as I approached. It sat for a moment or two, and then flew off into the night.

A few hundred yards on, and a badger ran out in front of me – the first I have actually seen since we moved. These are the famous aquatic badgers of the Somerset Levels – they forsake woods and fields for this damp wetland habitat. After running along for a few moments, it plunged into the ditch and disappeared.

Then, as I turned the corner to lead back up the main road, a second Barn Owl – again, perched on a roadside post. It sat and watched me, then flew up – but instead of flying off into the night, it hovered momentarily on soft, silent wings before plummeting down after a vole and melting away into the darkness.

September

Meare Heath

For over a year, since we first moved down to Somerset, I have failed in my quest to see one of Britain's most sought after and delightful mammals. Today, after many frustrating attempts, I finally succeeded.

It was one of those moments when your mouth acts quicker than your brain. The shout of 'Otter!' came before I had really realised what I was looking at. Something about the way the sleek, smooth shape broke the surface of the water triggered my subconscious, and before the creature had the chance to submerge again I had called out its name.

I was particularly pleased, as my companion was Simon Nash, chief executive of the Somerset Wildlife Trust. Simon has not been in the post all that long, but he and his colleagues have utterly transformed this organisation into one of the leading wildlife trusts in the country, with more than 20,000 members.

He sees great potential in the extraordinary range of habitats and wildlife that Somerset has to offer, and perhaps feels that the county has been overlooked in the past compared to better-known West Country wildlife hotspots such as Dorset, Devon and Cornwall. But as he says, the combination of Exmoor, the Quantocks, the Mendips and the Somerset Levels is a hard one to beat.

For a few minutes after we spotted the Otter, we were treated to splendid views of this large, dog-like animal seemingly playing with the fish that were concentrated in the pool. As they leapt into the air, frantically breaking the surface, a trail of bubbles followed them. From time to time, the head, back or tail of the Otter would appear, then disappear again.

Otters were once common on the Somerset Levels, but decades of pollution and persecution almost drove them to extinction in this part of the country. In the past, in Scotland, I have sometimes watched Otters on the coast, where their habits make them easier to see. But this was the first I have ever seen in this area – and a very welcome sight.

SUNDAY 23 SEPTEMBER

Bike ride from Mark to Glastonbury and back

I do occasionally go into the countryside with a purpose other than watching birds, and this Sunday morning I cycled to Glastonbury and back with an old friend, Simon Humphries.

Nevertheless, I couldn't resist taking my binoculars, and was glad that I did. For our route passed right through my favourite local birding spot, Shapwick and Meare Heaths, where we rode along the disused railway path.

It didn't take much to persuade Simon to take a break, so we spent a few minutes in the hide overlooking Noah's Lake. Mute Swans were everywhere – more than 150 of them scattered across the water – though a large bird of prey quartering the reeds, its chocolate-brown plumage set off by a creamy crown, was a less predictable sight. It was a female Marsh Harrier, which has been hanging around the area for a couple of months now.

On the way home we glimpsed a flash of blue along a rhyne near Godney, a brief and frustrating view of one of the local Kingfishers. We also saw a tiny little bird: looking like a plump, short-tailed Robin, with a dark brown head and white patches on the wings. It was the first Stonechat I have seen this autumn, and is likely to spend the next few months here, feeding on the tiny insects which can survive in our relatively mild winter climate.

These sightings were a useful reminder that a bicycle is not only more environmentally friendly than the car, but also a much better way to see birds!

SUNDAY 30 SEPTEMBER

Steart Point, Somerset

With Suzanne and the children away at her parents, I took the chance to spend a leisurely morning birding on the other side of the River Parrett, at Steart Point. Timing is essential here: an hour before high tide, and a couple of hours afterwards, are the perfect time to see hordes of migrant waders as they fuel up on the edge of the Severn estuary before heading south.

As I approached the tower hide, a flock of waders was flushed by a party of birders ahead of me, momentarily filling the skies with the beating of their wings, then coming down to earth again. As I got closer, I could see more than 500 Curlews, plus a few Bar-tailed Godwits, huddled together at the edge of the saltmarsh. Behind them, well over a thousand Shelduck – huge white ducks with dark heads and bright red bills – were floating on the sea.

From the hide itself, I could see a really good selection of waders of more than a dozen different species, each feeding or roosting in the area appropriate to them. On the shallow pools, Ruff, Redshank and Greenshank; along the river itself, a dozen Avocets; and in the fields around, hundreds of Lapwings, wheeling into the sky when a Peregrine passed by, uttering their evocative squealing cries.

A closer look through the telescope revealed half a dozen tiny waders picking morsels of food with their beaks: our smallest wader, the Little Stint. Barely the size of a sparrow, these tiny waders undertake an incredible journey each autumn, south and west from their breeding grounds in the far north of Scandinavia and northern Russia. They stop off for a few days or weeks here on the Severn estuary, building up their fat reserves, before continuing south to spend the winter in sub-Saharan Africa.

Five of the birds were clearly juveniles: their fresh plumage and the white Vs on their backs visible even at this distance. The other was an adult, which a hopeful birder in the hide was trying, without success, to turn into the Little Stint's rare American relative, the Semi-palmated Sandpiper. Personally, I was simply happy to marvel, once again, at the miracle of migration.

In the garden

It has been a quiet start to the month, with largely fine weather and few special birds, apart from a Long-tailed Tit and a calling Tawny Owl.

Lots of Swallows overhead still; and singing Robins are busily defending their autumn territory.

On a bright, clear morning in the middle of the month an adult Hobby flew low overhead, chasing (but failing to catch) the Swallows. The first Grey Wagtail of the year – almost a month earlier than last autumn – also flew over the house, calling.

Last year a pair of these birds spent a month or so with us during the late autumn, and gave wonderful views as they perched on the tiled roof of our outhouse to feed on insects there. I remember seeing one bird perched right next to a patch of mustard-yellow lichen, which almost perfectly mimicked the wagtail's lemon belly.

One evening in the middle of this month, my friend and former colleague Chris Baines paid us a flying visit in the company of a friend who lives in south Somerset. Back in the 1970s Chris virtually invented wildlife gardening, so it was both a pleasure and a slightly nerve-wracking experience to show him around the back garden.

He was suitably impressed, and his expert eyes opened mine to the potential we have here to create something truly special for wildlife. Maybe in a few years, when the children are older and we have more time, we can have a proper go.

A cool breeze that evening, and the first signs of a passage of migrating Swallows overhead. The following few mornings I went out early, and was rewarded by a few calling pipits overhead. The migrating Swallows were joined by House Martins, and larger flocks of Starlings at morning and evening.

Yet the mild weather meant that not just Robins, but Wrens and Dunnocks were all singing, the Dunnocks performing a duet with their persistent (and rather annoying) call.

And at the end of the month, the annual invasion of Pied Wagtails began: having been only occasional visitors during the summer, they returned in force, hunting for insects on our roofs and those of Rick's farmyard buildings. Pied Wagtails are one of the most overlooked yet attractive of all our common garden birds, so it was a treat to see them here again.

October

Kingsway, Mark

We were on our way to drop the children off at nursery this morning, when a small, slender furry creature ran across the road in front of the car and into the grassy bank. In London there could only be one possible candidate: a grey squirrel. But here in the countryside squirrels are mercifully scarce; and besides, this was much smaller and slimmer, with a white front and brown back.

It was, of course, a Stoat: the mammal that, pound for pound, is probably our most fearsome predator. I have seen film of a stoat killing a rabbit that weighs perhaps twice as much as it does, then dragging the dead animal back into a safe place to devour it, though we weren't treated to quite such a display from this elusive individual.

Charlie, unduly influenced by *The Wind in the Willows*, is convinced that what we saw was a weasel, and indeed the two creatures are not always all that easy to tell apart – the black tip to the stoat's tail as it disappears into the vegetation by the side of the road being the best field mark.

Other mammals which I regularly come across include fox and badger. But what a difference between the urban foxes I have been used to and these retiring rural creatures!

Back in the summer I stumbled across an adult fox with a cub in the long grass in our garden meadow. Whereas in London the animal would have faced me down with an arrogant, unblinking stare, these creatures bolted as soon as they realised I was there.

The local badgers are just as furtive, though not because of any particular shyness, but due to their nocturnal habits. Having found the badger trail earlier in the year, we are now suffering the effects of their messy feeding habits. First, holes all over the front and back lawns – intriguing for Charlie, George and Daisy, but just plain annoying for us. Then, the raiding of a plastic tub in which I keep premium quality bird seed. It's bad enough having to pay a fortune for this stuff (though as the birds love it I am not too resentful); when it gets wolfed down by an animal I haven't even seen yet I start to get a bit cross!

FRIDAY 5 – SUNDAY 7 OCTOBER

Mill Batch

One of the best things about having moved down to Somerset is that people drop in to visit us, either because they are eager to get their 'fix' of the countryside, or simply because they are passing through. This weekend we have had several visitors, including the artist Chris Rose.

Chris is one of my favourite bird artists – for both his work and his company. Although I have known him for ten years or so, until now we have only ever met either at the Birdfair or at the Society of Wildlife Artists' annual reception. Neither of these functions is designed to allow lengthy conversation, so when Chris mentioned that he would be passing by on the way back to his home on the Scottish borders, we were delighted.

Like me, Chris grew up on the outskirts of London during the 1960s and 1970s; indeed, given that he lived just a few miles down the road I am amazed that we never met as youngsters.

Unlike me, Chris has an extraordinary talent for painting: his pictures are quite unmistakable; he creates images with a burning intensity. I wish we could afford his originals, but we have to settle for two wonderful prints instead.

One depicts an autumnal scene: a flock of Hawfinches, Redwings and Fieldfares feeding on the forest floor, in late afternoon light. The birds simply glow – their colours honed to a perfect verisimilitude by Chris's expert brush.

The other print presents some of our visitors with a bit of a puzzle, as it appears to be a very well executed picture of a large, leafy plant (Butterbur, for the expert botanists). After a minute or two, they usually spot the real focus of the painting: a tiny Whitethroat, nestling in the shade of one of the enormous leaves.

These are the two things I love about Chris's paintings. First, the almost luminous quality he manages to give his subjects. Second, the way he sees birds: not always in the conventional way, and allowing you to notice something new every time you look.

As a person, Chris is far from the usual image of the intense, tortured artist: a tall, convivial man who is amazingly tolerant of our rather active children. Actually almost all the bird artists I know are pretty laid back. They manage to combine great passion for their art and for their subjects with a friendly, equable attitude to life as a whole.

We spent a very enjoyable evening discussing birds, birding and art. Typically, Suzanne asked the killer question: 'How do you *feel* when you paint birds?' Chris was, for once, stumped for words. With paintings like his, he didn't really need to find an answer.

Earlier this weekend, David and Martine Osorio spent a couple of nights with us. They are the parents of my school friend and longest-standing birding companion Daniel and, for a period in the 1970s, virtually became my adoptive parents – at least during the school holidays.

I am an only child, while Daniel is the eldest of four. To David and Martine, having an extra child around wasn't really an issue, so from about 1973 until 1977 I simply tagged along on their family holidays.

The Osorios had a simple and practical philosophy: that one good turn deserves another. During the year, they welcomed friends from outside London into their large, rambling home in Teddington. In return, during the school holidays, they would pile themselves, four children and me into a Dormobile van, and go off to stay with various families up and down the country.

Our first trip was in October 1973, to North Norfolk, an event I chronicled in *This Birding Life*. After that we went to the Scottish borders, Dorset, back to Norfolk, and various other parts of the country. Daniel and I visited places – and saw birds – we could only dream of.

But much more importantly than that, David and Martine gave me something I really needed. As a rather spoilt only child, I had to learn what family life was really like. Spending time with them and Daniel's younger siblings, Rachel, Thomas and Jessica, knocked the corners off me, and gave me the experience of living with other people, which I now truly appreciate.

They also gave us all independence – something I talked to Martine about this weekend. Looking back, I find it astonishing that she allowed her son – and by default, me – to hitchhike along the North Norfolk coast, cycle to the New Forest, and spend day after day from dawn to dusk watching birds, all before we reached the age of 15. My mother would never have let me do these things without David and Martine's approval; but because they thought it was OK, she gave her permission.

So I have a lot to thank them for – and it was wonderful to be able to return a tiny portion of the kindness and hospitality they have shown me over the years, by having them to stay at Mill Batch. Even if, as Martine reminded me as she left, they did bring supper for all of us on the first night!

Meare Heath

A famous Scottish birder used to divide his fellow enthusiasts into 'arsers' and 'leggers'. The latter would race around from one place to another, trying to cover as much ground as possible, so he could see the maximum number of different birds. The former would stay put in a single spot, and wait for the birds to come to him, on the principle that staying in one place often yields the best results.

I must confess that my natural impatience usually puts me in the leggers' camp. But sometimes, hanging around brings unexpected dividends. Even if, in this case, I didn't get to see the bird I was waiting for.

Back in September I had heard that a Purple Heron – a rare visitor from southern Europe – had been seen at Meare Heath, a few miles from my home. True to form, this was a very elusive bird. It would spend most of the day hidden in reeds, only showing itself when taking a short flight to another part of the reedbed.

By the last week of September, the large pool to the north of the footpath had been drained, providing the ideal home for various wading birds – including, I hoped, the Purple Heron.

In early October a second pool was drained, creating even more suitable habitat. And sure enough, sightings of the heron began to increase – with a few lucky birders even seeing it feeding out in the open.

So today I decided that a spot of 'arsing' was the only option. Staying in one place for over two hours might give me a chance of seeing this frustrating bird. And this morning, before heading off to work, I did just that.

My first surprise was the sheer numbers of another member of the heron family. Almost fifty Little Egrets lined up along the banks of the pool, like ballerinas waiting to go on stage. With them were several Grey Herons, the Purple Heron's larger relative. But still no sign of the bird itself.

As the mist cleared, shapes began to come into view. Two large, long-legged, rather ungainly waders – a pair of Ruff. Several Snipe, probing the soft mud with their long bills. And a small, neat, almost black-and-white bird – a Green Sandpiper – stopping off en route from its Scandinavian breeding grounds to spend the winter south of the Sahara.

Then there was a pair of Kingfishers, chasing each other back and forth across the pool, before plunging into the reeds.

Best of all, a Pectoral Sandpiper, a medium-sized North American wader with a distinctive streaked breast pattern which gives the species its name. Pectoral Sandpipers occasionally go off course on their journey south from Arctic Canada to South America, fly across the Atlantic, and end up here in Britain. Not a bird I would have seen if I had simply scanned the pool and walked on by.

After two hours, with no sign of the Purple Heron, I gave up. But given what I did manage to see, there might be something to be said for hanging around in one place . . .

Meare Heath

Dropping in again on my way home this afternoon, in another vain attempt to see the Purple Heron, I gained two minor rewards. First, a lone Jay flying in the far distance – believe it or not the very first I have seen in this part of Somerset since my move down here. (Trees are few and far between in these parts . . .)

Then, as I was scanning through the Lapwings and gulls as they flew up from the drained pool, another bird caught my eye. Lighter both in plumage and movement, with an ethereal, buoyant flight, I realised immediately it was something special. The pale grey plumage, and dark markings on the cap and neck, marked it out as a Black Tern in non-breeding plumage.

Black Terns don't breed in Britain, so this bird had either come from Eastern Europe or, more likely, the Netherlands. Like the Little Stints I saw last month at Steart, it's another passage migrant, passing through Britain on its way to spend the winter in Africa.

Back in mid-September 1974, on a blustery day at my old stomping ground, Staines Reservoirs, about 180 Black Terns delighted a large crowd of birders – including Daniel and me – as they swooped over the water. Seeing this single bird wasn't quite as spectacular, but was nevertheless an unexpected and very welcome surprise.

Having hassled a Teal, and been chased in turn by the Lapwings, it was on its way again – a brief but memorable moment, and further compensation for failing yet again to seen this blasted heron!

In the garden

Another quiet start to the month, though the mild, damp mornings meant that we often woke to an autumnal chorus of birdsong, from the local Robins, Wrens and Starlings.

It has often been said that the only bird to sing during the autumn and winter months is the Robin – the likely identity of the famous 'Nightingale' that supposedly sang in Berkeley Square. But in fact you can hear quite a few species singing out of season, including the odd Chiffchaff, which seem to enjoy uttering their name on fine, sunny days during September and October.

Chiffchaffs are now wintering in Britain in quite good numbers, as they can survive by hunting out tiny insects on foliage in much the same way as Goldcrests and Long-tailed Tits. But birds which need to feed on *flying* insects simply can't endure even the mildest winter, so this month we've seen the final departure, for another year, of the local Swallows.

The bulk of the village Swallows departed in the third week of September, with small parties of migrating birds passing over until the end of that month. The last one flew over our garden on 3 October, looking rather lonely as it headed south.

House Martins stay a bit longer than the Swallows, but even so, I was surprised to see a flock of about 15 hawking for insects in the morning drizzle on 13 October. Just to add to the seasonal confusion, the Fieldfares and Redwings have arrived for the winter, with small flocks of both species feasting on what is left of our hawthorn and elder berries.

On 5 October the weather turned bright and chilly for the first time this autumn, and not surprisingly bird activity picked up. We don't really live on a migration route, but nevertheless I noticed a few Meadow Pipits overhead, while Goldcrests have recolonised the giant conifer in our next-door neighbour's garden.

It used to be thought that Goldcrests were far too frail to attempt a sea crossing, so when large numbers turned up each autumn on our eastern coasts, it was assumed they had hitched a lift from Scandinavia on the backs of birds such as Short-eared Owls!

The truth is even more extraordinary: despite weighing only five or so grams (about the weight of a 20 pence coin, or a single sheet of A4 paper), these little mites are able to make a crossing of the North Sea, at night, and find their way to the safety of landfall by dawn.

The same morning saw a new addition to the garden list. At first I ignored the strange deep croaking sound coming from the orchard next door, dismissing it as just another Rook or Carrion Crow. But as it persisted, it occurred to me that a larger member of the corvid tribe might be responsible. Sure enough, sitting in one of the apple trees, and dwarfing a small flock of Jackdaws, was a large, black crow with a huge bill and shaggy feathering around the neck: a Raven.

Ravens are doing rather well in this neck of the woods: or at least on the higher ground nearby. They nest in some of the quarries on the Mendips, and a wildlife cameraman I know, Ian McCarthy, has even noticed them on the village green at Shirehampton, a suburb of Bristol.

Not all that long ago they were confined to hilly and mountainous parts of Britain, where they had been driven by persecution. But now that they are at least tolerated by farmers, if not exactly welcomed, they are spreading eastwards and colonising lowland parts of the country.

Later that day, when things warmed up, I was treated to the incongruous sight of flocks of Starlings hawking for insects in the sunny, blue sky above the garden. They took on an almost balletic quality as they swooped around, stopping every few seconds to grab another beakful of insects.

Down in the garden itself, lots more insect activity: Common Darter dragonflies, along with Peacock, Small Tortoiseshell and

Speckled Wood butterflies. The summer that left us back in April appears to be returning in this dry, warm October!

Something rather bizarre has been happening recently. Around the middle of the morning, from somewhere very near the house, comes the unmistakable hooting of a Tawny Owl. I first heard it last December, and wondered at the time if someone was using a tape recording to play a trick on me. Suzanne heard it again this month, and later on, so did I. Tawny Owls do call much more at this time of year, because the youngsters are trying to muscle in on their parents' territories; but even so, a regular daylight caller is unusual, to say the least.

THURSDAY 18 – FRIDAY 19 OCTOBER

North Norfolk

Good weather is something of a mixed blessing for birders. Nobody likes wind and rain, but such conditions often bring the best birds – especially in autumn, when passing migrants may be grounded by bad weather.

So when my first day in Norfolk dawned fine, clear and dry, I knew we were going to have to work hard to see anything interesting. Nevertheless I was glad to be out of the office for a day or two, and free from the shackles of e-mails and meetings.

I have been coming to Norfolk for 35 years now, and since my very first visit as an impressionable teenager in October 1973 I have had some wonderful birding experiences here. From flocks of winter thrushes flying overhead in autumn, to skeins of noisy Pink-footed Geese in winter; and from flocks of waders migrating northwards in spring, to rare breeding birds like Golden Orioles and Montagu's Harriers in summer, Norfolk rarely fails to deliver.

*

My companions on this October day were Martin Woodcock (can you imagine a more appropriate name for one of Britain's top bird artists?) and his wife Barbara. I had known of Martin for many years before we actually met – as the illustrator of a host of field guides, and the epic, multi-volume *Birds of Africa* – but was utterly unprepared for the man himself.

Given his exalted place in the pantheon of world ornithology, I never expected that he would be so kind, funny and dry-witted; wonderful company both in the field and over a glass of fine red wine in the evenings after birding.

Barbara is equally charming, welcoming me as always into their home with her customary hospitality. So as we set forth on a fine October morning, in truth I wasn't all that bothered about the birds – I knew we were going to have an enjoyable day out anyway.

We parked along Lady Anne's Drive and walked towards the vast pine woods that stretch along this part of the coast, providing an important windbreak for the land behind the dunes. I'm always amazed that anyone ever finds a bird in this impenetrable mass of conifers, but every autumn the woods play host to all sorts of goodies from Asia: tiny warblers that by rights should be sunning themselves somewhere in the Far East – not shivering in a Norfolk woodland.

The woods had been full of birds the day before (the usual story), but were now very quiet. With persistence, we did catch a brief glimpse of a Yellow-browed Warbler, a rare visitor from Siberia. As always, I marvelled at how a bird barely larger than a Goldcrest can travel thousands of miles to end up on our shores – and still be as skulking and elusive as ever.

Martin and Barbara reckoned that Titchwell would be a better bet – and they were right. After a satisfying lunch at the Lord Nelson pub in Burnham Thorpe, we headed westwards along the coast to this show-piece RSPB reserve.

The wind dropped, the sun shone, and as we walked along the

footpath from the car park to the coast we were joined by dozens of other birders, dog walkers and people just out to enjoy a pleasant stroll.

Titchwell is one of my favourite birding haunts, mainly because it is designed to make life easier for me and my fellow enthusiasts. The lagoons are to the east of the path, with spacious, large-windowed hides facing out towards them, which means that by early afternoon the light is behind you, illuminating the birds on view.

The main lagoon held a good range of waders, including a Little Stint, which had stopped off at Titchwell to refuel on its journey from the Arctic to Africa.

As we wandered down towards the beach, a larger wader caught my eye as it waded waist-deep in the water. A Spotted Redshank – longer-billed and altogether more elegant than its commoner relative – fed only a few yards away from us. This attractive, tundra-nesting bird may have been on its way to Africa, or may simply decide to spend the winter on a south coast estuary, where a few linger each year.

While watching the Spotted Redshank, I became aware of a fellow birder looking intently at me. As he greeted me with a familiar hello, I peered beneath his headgear and realised that it was an old colleague of mine, Matthew, who now works at the BBC in Glasgow.

With him were his wife and son Oscar – whom I recall meeting a few years ago, and who has developed a keen interest in birds, partly thanks to a bird book I gave him at the time. It was good to see that having reached his teenage years Oscar was still an active birder, as so many young people lose their interest as they reach this period in their life.

Early next morning, Martin and I made a quick jaunt to Cley – once memorably described as 'Mecca for birders'. Ever since I first came here with my friend Daniel back in autumn 1973, it has been one of my favourite places; and as the sun shone on the reeds, making them glow with golden intensity, I couldn't think of anywhere I would rather be.

We parked by the new visitor centre, a building viewed by Martin, to quote Prince Charles's famous words, as a 'monstrous carbuncle on the face of a much-loved friend' – the friend, in this case, being the unique North Norfolk landscape.

Swiftly moving on, we headed towards the trio of hides in the centre of the reserve. As we scanned the lagoons in front of our hide, Martin noticed a small, dark, streaky bird feeding amongst the ducks and waders. It was a Rock Pipit, the only British songbird to live exclusively on our coasts. But apart from the pipit, things seemed pretty quiet.

Then, as I looked over towards the distant reedbed, a dozen or more tiny, long-tailed birds shot up from the reeds, hung in the air, then plunged down again. Bearded Tits!

They had been flushed from their reedy hiding-place by a passing Marsh Harrier, and as it flew over they spooked again, flying right over us. Stepping out of the hide, I could hear their characteristic metallic pinging calls: they were very close indeed.

As I waited, there was a movement a few feet in front of me, and a stunning male Bearded Tit appeared, clinging to the reed. Then another, together with several females and juveniles. The males were simply breathtaking: with blue-grey heads, orangey-buff plumage and the jet-black markings to either side of their bills that give the species its name.

Later, Martin told me that these blue and orange shades are opposite each other on the artist's colour spectrum, so complement each other perfectly. But for now, all I could do was marvel at the sheer beauty of the bird – and be grateful for the bright, windless day that showed it off to perfection.

My visit to Norfolk was over all too soon. As always, there was not nearly enough time for watching birds; nor to visit some of my birding friends who have settled along this famous stretch of coast – including Robert Gillmor, whose fine artwork graces the cover of this book. But what I love about Norfolk is that it is impossible to exhaust its possibilities for seeing great birds, and meeting fellow birders, so there is always an excuse to come back.

SUNDAY 28 OCTOBER

Weston-super-Mare

A trip to the cinema with the whole family, including my elder sons James and David, David's girlfriend Katie, and our friend Graham. We had come to see the new animated feature *Ratatouille*, and were rather nervous – Charlie had been to the pictures before, but would George and Daisy, who are not yet three, cope with a full-length film on the big screen?

In the event, Charlie enjoyed the story, Daisy was captivated by the colours and action, and George . . . well, George knows what he likes, and he liked the rat. 'Anything else, George?' 'Just the rat.'

As we returned to the car park, groups of tiny birds were flitting from tree to tree, calling as they went. For a brief moment I mistook them for Long-tailed Tits, which usually travel in small flocks. But I soon realised my error: they were Pied Wagtails, using the ornamental trees around the car park as a place to roost. For a few minutes we all stood and watched them as they zipped around this concrete desert, their high-pitched contact calls filling the evening air.

Why these little birds should gather in places like this would baffle most people. But the answer is simple. Shopping centres, service stations and industrial estates – the Pied Wagtails' favourite roost sites – are generally well-lit and a bit warmer than the surrounding countryside.

So the birds gain two benefits: they are safe from the attention of nocturnal predators, and by huddling together in a marginally warmer environment, are better able to conserve energy on cold winter nights.

*

A few years ago I filmed the wagtail roost in the centre of the Devon town of Newton Abbot, for a series with Bill Oddie. We were amazed at how so few passers-by bothered to stop and look at the incredible sight of about 400 birds roosting in a single tree, outside Marks and Spencer. I'm often intrigued at how some people appear to be 'bird-blind', and in this case 'bird-deaf' as well!

Even my two elder sons, David and James (who have a pathological lack of interest in all things feathered) were impressed by the incongruity of seeing the wagtails flitting around a car park in the middle of Weston-super-Mare. Who knows, they might become birders yet . . .

MONDAY 29 OCTOBER

Kennard Moor and Meare Heath

A week off work, to catch up with various things to do around the house and garden. So as Monday dawned fine and sunny, what better opportunity to go birding?! Fortunately I had the perfect excuse: Graham had been staying for the weekend and was returning to London that afternoon, so this was our last chance to see a few birds.

We headed out to Kennard Moor, just south of Glastonbury Tor, where no fewer than three Great Bustards had been reported during the past week or so. You wouldn't think birds of this size could easily disappear, but believe me, they can. So we joined forces with a fellow birder and began methodically scanning the area with our binoculars.

Eventually, after a few minutes, the bustards flew in from the back of the moor, landed and immediately began to feed.

Of course these are not truly wild birds, having dispersed here from the reintroduction scheme on Salisbury Plain. Beryl, the bird I saw back in January, was here, still wearing her orange wingtag, number 15.

Beryl had brought along two other females, each bearing a yellow

wingtag (numbers 18 and 22). These are, I learned from the SOS website, a year younger than her, so perhaps they have followed her to take
advantage of her greater experience of finding food during the autumn
and winter.

Kennard Moor is one of those lovely spots that seem to act as a magnet
for birds, even in this area of prime habitat. One local birder, Gerry
Urch, watches the place every day, and is justly rewarded with some
really good sightings. These include a Great Grey Shrike, which I have
yet to catch up with: a winter visitor from the east that is growing
increasingly scarce in Britain.

On this particular day we missed the shrike, but were compensated
in the form of a splendid male Merlin, which perched momentarily on
top of a tree; two Little Owls, soaking up the autumn sunshine in the
knot-hole of a gnarled old oak; and best of all, a singing male Pied
Wagtail on a gate right beside us. Sometimes it's the unexpected behaviour of the commonest bird which delights you more than a rarity, and
this was just such an occurrence.

With an hour or so to spare before we had to return home (where my
eldest son David was kindly babysitting the younger trio), we dropped
in to Meare Heath, my regular patch.

Once again, we didn't see the elusive Purple Heron, but this was
one of those mornings where it really didn't matter. The drained pool
was covered with birds: several hundred Lapwings, along with a couple
of Ruff and a lone Black-tailed Godwit.

As we stood around, we saw a smart male Stonechat perched on top
of a bramble bush, his orange breast set off by his dark brown head.
We also enjoyed several sightings of Kingfishers, and heard at least
two singing Chiffchaffs. From Noah's Hide we had good views of a
female Marsh Harrier, followed by a distant male over the reedbed by
the drained pool.

By now the footpath which runs along the edge of the pools had filled up with people: some were birders; others simply fancied a walk in the countryside on a fine autumn day. As we were about to head home, we heard a distinctive, slow beating of wings. Looking up we saw a family party of three Whooper Swans, which landed right in front of us, much to the discomfort of the Lapwing flock. Unlike Mute Swans, juvenile Whoopers are pure white by now, having moulted before they set off on their migration.

These three beautiful creatures had, we knew, just travelled all the way from Iceland to our little corner of Somerset.

November

Westhay

With Charlie, George and Daisy in tow, I checked out the Starling roost at Westhay for my colleagues at *Autumnwatch*. In fact I was pretty sure the birds were gathering a few miles down the road at Shapwick, but it was a nice evening, and the children needed some fresh air.

On the way, I stopped briefly at a reed-fringed pool on which some Teal were feeding, along with no fewer than four Green Sandpipers. Green Sandpiper is one of my favourite waders: neat, almost black-and-white, with a distinctive flight action in which it whirs along on stiff wings. They have come here all the way from Scandinavia – perhaps even farther east – and may be going all the way to Africa; though, like so many waders, they appear to be changing their migratory habits and spending the winter right here in Britain.

At the roost itself, it was all a bit of an anti-climax. There were hardly any Starlings, though hundreds of Redwings and Fieldfares overhead reminded me what a good autumn it has been for these two species.

One small fly in the ointment: a bright, new 4x4 vehicle, emblazoned with the logo of the Volvo Round-the-World Yacht Race, was parked along the drove – despite the very obvious car park where everyone else had left their cars. I politely pointed out to the driver that cars aren't really allowed here; to which I got the reply, 'Oh, we're regulars here, and we're RSPB members, you know.'

Resisting the temptation to point out that this is in fact a Somerset Wildlife Trust reserve, and that being an RSPB member does not immediately grant you the right to park your car wherever you like, I shrugged my shoulders and moved on.

SATURDAY 3 NOVEMBER

Kennard Moor

Another outing with George and Daisy, to Kennard Moor, in search of the Great Grey Shrike. This is a really scarce bird, so worth a special trip.

Unfortunately, I was about half an hour too late. On the way I met a fellow birder who told me he had just seen the shrike chasing a butterfly; by the time we arrived, the bird had gone.

Shapwick and Meare Heaths

Simon King and the *Autumnwatch* team are spending a couple of nights back on Simon's home turf to broadcast live from the Starling roost. It was good to catch up with Simon and some other old friends as they prepared for the night's filming.

Their presence here, announced on the previous night's show, attracted several hundred people – ranging from hardcore birders to curious locals – who lined the drove where the best views can usually be had. I wandered down to the hide, and enjoyed the sight of fairly large flocks of Starlings coming in – though nothing like the numbers we hope to see later in the winter.

As dusk fell, and the rest of the people wandered away, I was rewarded for my persistence by a distant Bittern flapping low over the reedbed. I went home happy – especially in the knowledge that I could watch the programme in the comfort of my sitting room and not have to stay out in the freezing Somerset night.

Greylake RSPB Reserve, Somerset

Yet another outing *'con bambini'* – once again, with George and Daisy. This time we were visiting the new RSPB reserve at Greylake, in the southern part of the Somerset Levels, half an hour's drive from home. This is another piece of wetland habitat which the RSPB are hoping to turn into a showpiece reserve. So far, it has already started to attract some excellent birds – and, as a consequence, birders.

Today we had a very clear target: a Glossy Ibis, a rare wanderer from southern Europe, which turned up here earlier this week. This is a long-legged, rather prehistoric-looking bird: about three feet tall, with a brownish plumage (not much gloss on this particular bird) and a huge, decurved bill.

Fortunately, given the limited attention span of a pair of two-year olds, the ibis was remarkably obliging, feeding only a few yards away from the boardwalk, very near the reserve entrance.

Showing some promise as a birder, George declared it to be a heron, while Daisy clearly wasn't really terribly interested, given that it wasn't pink. A flamingo would be ideal, I suppose . . .

WEDNESDAY 14 NOVEMBER

Berrow Beach

A rather frustrating pre-work trip to Berrow Beach, in search of a storm-driven Grey Phalarope reported yesterday. Apparently the bird, driven onshore by strong westerly winds, allowed a local birder to get within a few feet as it swam on a tiny pool left by the receding tide.

The resulting photos posted on the SOS website were truly jaw-dropping: an instant confirmation of the bird's presence. Yet it isn't all that long ago – before the age of digital photography – that we would have had to wait a couple of months to see pictures of a rarity like this in one of the birding magazines.

By the next morning, however, it had gone, and my visit was made even more frustrating by the presence of two huge, black, Rottweiler-type dogs bounding along the shoreline and panicking a flock of 1500 or so Dunlin.

Most dog walkers on this beach are pretty responsible, either keeping their pets on leads or making sure that they don't frighten the birds. These owners appeared to have vanished, so the dogs ran riot.

For the poor birds, some of which may have flown here all the way from the Arctic and be in urgent need of nourishment, this was an unwelcome distraction from the important business of feeding. The intricate patterns they made while swirling around the sky were poor compensation for the knowledge that some may die of hunger as a result of the disturbance.

THURSDAY 15 NOVEMBER

Mill Batch

Another old friend comes to stay, but this time from farther afield. Marek Borkowski is over from Poland on his annual lecture tour and drops in for the night between speaking engagements.

Marek is one of the great pioneers of birding in Eastern Europe, and a truly extraordinary man. His gigantic bushy beard and four delightful children are a famous feature of the Birdfair, where his Birding Poland stand attracts hundreds of visitors every year. Many take up the option of visiting Poland on one of Marek's guided tours, and are never disappointed.

Marek and I sat and watched the final episode of *Autumnwatch*, which even by the usual standards got a little bit silly. First, we had 'duck-cam' – a failed attempt to get close to ducks roosting on the lake at Martin Mere. Then, as he watched Bill Oddie and Kate Humble impersonating beavers, Marek turned to me and, in a solemn tone, uttered his considered verdict: 'We don't have anything like this on Polish television.'

SATURDAY 24 NOVEMBER

Mill Batch

The coldest morning of the autumn so far, with a sharp frost. I had forgotten to refill the bird feeders, and the bird bath was covered with ice, so George, Daisy and I ventured outside to sort things out.

As soon as the feeders were replenished, the birds arrived: first a Robin, then Blue and Great Tits, and finally the finches. I took advantage of the good light to point out the differences between the Blue Tit and Great Tit, but I'm not sure the children took much notice – they were too busy peering at the broken ice salvaged from the bird bath, and watching with wide, astonished eyes as it melted in front of their eyes.

FRIDAY 25 NOVEMBER

Cheddar Reservoir

The SOS website announced the presence of a Red-necked Grebe at Cheddar Reservoir. Given that this is a relatively scarce visitor to these parts, it seemed too good an opportunity to miss, so I headed up there, this time just with George in tow.

As we arrived, he announced, with the determined certainty of a two year old, that he wanted to feed the ducks. I was lacking the main requirement for this – bread – and besides, a quick scan had revealed that the grebe was nowhere in sight.

Seeing some sheep along the path that runs around the reservoir rim, I suggested that we go to see them instead – to which, fortunately, he acquiesced. George likes sheep (or 'sheeps', as he calls them with impeccable logic).

After we had gone a hundred yards or so, at George's pace rather than mine, we bumped into a couple of birders who did the usual 'you should have been here 20 minutes ago . . .' routine. Apparently a sailing boat had ventured rather close to the grebe, which promptly disappeared over the other side of the reservoir.

I scanned with my telescope, saw a couple of dozen Great Crested Grebes and about three thousand Coots in the distance, and realised that the only way I was going to see the rarer bird was to walk at least a third of the way around the reservoir's circumference.

Problem one: fading light; it was less than an hour before sunset. Problem two: George, who was very taken with the sheep. I have learned, the hard way, that the usual parental techniques of bribery, persuasion and threat rarely work with George, who has always had a very clear idea of what he wants to do. But fortunately the production of a banana (which I had hoped to eat myself, having missed lunch) seemed to work, and we started our long walk.

I managed to deflect his attention by pointing out the many Pied Wagtails that were flitting along the bank, though he took some persuading to admit that they were not Magpies. Gradually we got close to the area where the grebe had probably flown to, so from time to time I stopped to scan the reservoir.

Finally, as I panned yet again across the water, I noticed a smaller grebe, which immediately up-ended and dived. Things looked promising, although it took what seemed like an age (probably less than a minute) to surface again.

When it finally appeared, the slightly smaller size, darker neck and yellow bill all marked it out from its commoner relative. There was something about the shape and posture, too: a thicker, stiffer neck giving it a more compact 'jizz' – that indefinable quality by which an experienced birder knows that they are looking at something different.

By now, George had unilaterally decided that he was heading home, much to the amusement of a passing dog walker and a courting couple. I eventually caught him up, and the sheep diverted him long enough to get him back to the car park. He didn't actually see the Red-necked Grebe; but there's time for all that in future years. Next time I shall definitely remember to bring some bread . . .

Changes over time . . .

The library at work has had a clear-out, and one of the books on offer looked fascinating: *Somerset Birds and some other folk*, by E.W. Hendy, a popular nature writer of the first half of the 20th century.

I was immediately intrigued by the title of the opening chapter, *A Somerset Garden and its Birds*. Although the garden in question, at Porlock in the west of the county, was some distance from my own, the parallels and differences nevertheless made fascinating reading.

Hendy's garden would have been about the same size as ours – just over an acre – but there the similarities end. Whereas we are in the flatlands of the Somerset Levels, he was sandwiched between the coast and Exmoor, about 160 feet above sea level. And although many of the commoner birds he saw are still present in my own garden, several others are most certainly not.

Other things have hardly changed:

When breakfast is spread on lawn and table a swarm of small hungry people descends to feed. Blue and great tits squabble with each other on the table . . . greenfinches plop down solidly on the board and feed purposefully . . . chaffinches are more volatile . . . the pied wagtail flutters down from the roof like a shuttlecock . . . robins arrive with nerves all on edge . . . sparrows have no manners; they thrust and shove and elbow their way through the crowd and no-one, not even the gawky, rather stupid-looking song thrush, can turn them off.

(Interesting to note that the book was published during the Second World War, in 1944, yet Hendy still appears to have had enough food to spare his garden birds . . .)

But what wouldn't I give to enjoy the following experiences . . .?

Cirl buntings are very fond of bathing . . .

One summer, when a pair of nightingales had their nest near our garden, one of them frequently used our bird-bath, generally towards evening . . .

An open nesting box on the south side of our house is sometimes patronised by spotted flycatchers . . .

All three of these species have suffered major declines in numbers and range in the sixty years or so that separate Hendy's observations from my own. Spotted Flycatchers are still found in Somerset (see my encounter with a nesting pair back in June), but are much scarcer than they used to be. The same applies to Nightingales, which I have yet to hear since my move down here.

The third member of the trio, Cirl Bunting, was found patchily across the whole of southern England even when I first became aware of birds; but in the past three decades has retreated to a tiny area of south Devon, where farming and climatic conditions appear to favour the species. Indeed, thanks to sterling work by the RSPB and local farmers, the Cirl Bunting is actually extending its range. Who knows, in another thirty years we may see it back on the Polden Hills, just south of here.

December

O nce again, we have been enjoying unseasonably mild weather at the beginning of this month, with the thermometer peaking at almost 15 degrees – what used to be spring weather.

On quite a few days in recent weeks I have seen the Blue Tits going in and out of the nestbox by our kitchen window. Whether they are looking for a home for the coming spring, or simply a place to lodge when it gets cold this winter, is hard to say. The other problem is knowing whether it is the same bird – or the same pair – that I am seeing, or a succession of different birds.

This is also true of the birds visiting our feeders: studies have shown that if you see half a dozen Blue Tits at any one time, up to ten times as many – more than 50 birds in all – may actually be coming to your garden during the course of a winter's day.

This year I have read reports of the falling numbers of songbirds in our gardens. Correspondents to various newspapers and magazines have suggested that this is because populations of garden birds are declining. In fact many species – notably tits and finches – are doing rather well at the moment, despite what the doom-mongers would have you believe.

The real reason why there aren't many birds on our tables and feeders is simple: during spells of mild weather in autumn and winter there is still plenty of natural food available in the hedgerows and woods. As soon as it turns cold, they will head straight for the place they know they can be sure of a meal: our gardens.

In the local fields, Buzzards have begun to turn up in good numbers. At this time of year they can't take advantage of rising thermals of warm air to gain height, so they change their feeding strategy, and root around the muddy fields for earthworms. It always strikes me as odd to see this fine-looking bird of prey trudging around, the heavy soil sticking to its talons as it goes.

SUNDAY 2 DECEMBER

Burnham-on-Sea

The forecast said stormy weather, with gale force winds blowing straight up the Bristol Channel from the Atlantic Ocean. This time last year, similar conditions produced a 'wreck' of Leach's Petrels, one of the most sought-after of all our seabirds. So working on the principle that lightning does sometimes strike twice in the same place, I decided to go down to the nearest stretch of coastline to see what I could find.

I arrived at Burnham-on-Sea during a welcome break in the cloud cover, with shafts of sunshine lighting up the seafront. Burnham's pier is not the most impressive in the country – in fact it's not even the most impressive pier in Somerset – but it seemed like a good place to use as a watchpoint. By wedging myself into one corner of this dilapidated Victorian structure, I could gain some shelter from the gale, so I settled down for what might turn out to be a long and fruitless vigil.

As often happens in these parts, the water was remarkably devoid of birds. A few Oystercatchers stood along the tideline, hunched against the wind; a group of Shelduck battled westwards; and the odd gull flew past. But otherwise, all was quiet.

Then, as I struggled to keep my binoculars from shaking in the gusty breeze, I noticed a larger flock of gulls out to sea, dancing in the wind. Of all our gulls, only the Kittiwake has such a graceful, long-winged appearance, pearly-grey above and snow-white below, their wingtips looking as if they have been dipped in a pot of ink. They showed up beautifully: lit from the front but with dark clouds behind.

The Kittiwake is the most ocean-going of all our breeding gulls, spending much of the year out at sea. They breed on coastal cliffs, though they have adapted well to the modern world by nesting on man-made structures such as piers.

After breeding, Kittiwakes disperse around our coasts, though some travel much farther afield, ending up in such far-flung locations as Canada and West Africa. But despite their flying skills, stormy winds can easily catch them unawares and blow them off course.

Back in January, I found a Kittiwake a few miles from the coast, at Cheddar Reservoir, in quite a flustered state after being swept inland on strong winter gales.

Today, though, these birds were riding the winds like kids on a rollercoaster – and, as birds often do in such circumstances, looking like they were really enjoying themselves. Unfortunately, the hoped-for Leach's Petrels failed to appear; but as I packed away my telescope and headed home, I was consoled by the sight of the Kittiwake flock, still riding the wind currents despite the coming storm.

In the garden

Towards the end of the month, the long-awaited cold snap finally occurred, with the mercury dropping to seven degrees below zero one night. As predicted, the songbirds came back in force, with Great and Blue Tits, Greenfinches and Chaffinches competing to be the first to the feeders. A Song Thrush, a welcome sight nowadays, fed underneath, picking up dropped seeds.

In the week before Christmas, a party of Long-tailed Tits turned up outside the kitchen window and, for the first time since we moved here almost 18 months ago, actually visited the seed feeders. It's not all that long since Long-tailed Tits were recorded on artificial feeders for the very first time, but they seem to be quick learners, hanging on with their tiny claws and gorging themselves on the chopped sunflower hearts we provide.

Although they didn't stay around for long, I was still able to get a good look at them: noting the delicate combination of browns, creams and brownish-pinks that gives them such an attractive appearance.

Long-tailed Tits have all sorts of folk names, most of which are by now, sadly, obsolete. What a pity we no longer call these delightful little birds 'Kitty longtail', 'huckmuck', 'feather poke' or 'jug pot'! Apart from the first, these names don't refer to the bird, but to its extraordinary nest, a ball-like structure made from feathers, lichens and spider's webs.

The poet John Clare called Long-tailed Tits 'bumbarrels', also derived from the shape of their nest, although I like to think it is also a cheeky reference to the bird itself, which with its rounded body and long tail looks rather like a flying lollipop. The name features in the closing lines of one of my favourite of Clare's bird poems, a sonnet entitled 'Emmonsailes Heath in Winter':

> And coy bumbarrels twenty in a drove
> Flit down the hedgerow in the frozen plain
> And hang on little twigs and start again.

Cheddar Reservoir

Last week, when I saw a posting on the SOS website about a pair of Black-necked Grebes at Cheddar Reservoir, I decided to visit when I had a spare moment.

As I have already mentioned, Cheddar Reservoir is one of the most 'birder-friendly' of all the local sites, being somewhere you can pop in for 20 minutes or so and still have a sporting chance of seeing most of the birds there.

So imagine my surprise when two visits failed to produce the goods: several thousand Coots, a good selection of diving and dabbling ducks, and plenty of Great Crested Grebes – but absolutely no sign of their smaller relatives, the Black-necked Grebes.

On my third visit, on my way to work this morning, I was beginning to get annoyed. The website showed that the birds were an almost permanent presence, just off the Cheddar tower. On one of my visits someone had actually been watching them at virtually the same time as I was missing out – so what was going on?!

It was then that I realised my mistake. The instructions had said that the birds were being seen off the Cheddar tower, whereas I was at the opposite side, nearer the town of Axbridge. A swift drive around to the other side, and there they were: two Black-necked Grebes in their smart non-breeding plumage.

There are some species you always have a soft spot for, and Black-necked Grebe is one of mine. When I was growing up, this was one of our local specialities – usually seen at Staines Reservoirs in late August and early September, when the birds were moulting out of their breeding garb.

Even in winter they are a really attractive little bird: with a dark grey cap and neck, fluffy rear end and, most striking of all, a bright red eye.

They are about halfway in size and appearance between Little and Slavonian Grebes, but can generally be identified by a combination of plumage features and what birders call 'jizz'. Black-necked Grebes are stockier and less sleek than Slavonian Grebe (whose clean-cut, black and white plumage always reminds me of an auk such as a Guillemot), but noticeably larger than the Little Grebe. The other key feature, noticeable even at a great distance, is their short, slightly 'tip-tilted' bill.

These two were really close to the bank, and I spent a rewarding ten minutes or so watching them as they dived for food: launching themselves up into the air and then down into the water with their powerful legs, and then popping up like corks a few feet away. Then it was time to head off for work . . .

[Footnote: A few days later the following posting appeared on the SOS website:

No sighting this afternoon during a very quick scan, but watched an angler land a 12 lb Pike. The mouth was quite big enough to take a Little Grebe or Tufted Duck. I wonder how many ducks don't return to the surface after a dive. The largest pike that the fisherman had landed at Cheddar was 45 lb!]

SATURDAY 22 DECEMBER

Watchet Harbour, Somerset

My longest-standing birding friend Daniel is staying for a few days. I still think of him as my teenage birding buddy, which is a bit rich now that we are both pushing fifty. He is also incredibly important nowadays (I can hear a snort of derision as he reads this . . .), being a professor in the biology department at the University of Sussex and one of the world's leading experts in bird and insect vision. Tall, shambling and with a permanent look of surprised curiosity on his face, it is always a delight to have him to visit.

We first met back in September 1971, on our first day at Hampton Grammar School in West London. His surname is Osorio, and as there was no one in form 1J whose name began with 'N', we ended up sitting next to each other.

I don't know how we both realised we were birdwatchers. Actually, I do remember: it was at the end of that first week, and we were trudging off the rugby pitch covered in mud, when the subject came up. I think we knew we preferred birds to rugby (actually I prefer almost anything to *playing* rugby), and a few weeks later we arranged to meet at the weekend to go birding.

I can still recall my mother's panic as she discovered, too late, that Daniel was Jewish, and that the roast ham she was planning for lunch might not be a good idea. In the event, this wasn't an issue, and we began a friendship which has now lasted almost forty years.

Seeing that today is Daniel's birthday, I managed to negotiate an afternoon's birding while Suzanne looked after the children. Having completed our task of picking up some kitchen chairs from a furniture repairer in west Somerset, we headed back via the harbour at Watchet, a pleasant little seaside town along the coast towards Minehead.

We were hoping to see wintering Purple Sandpipers, an increasingly scarce bird in the south-west, but the tide was too far out, exposing acres of seaweed-covered rock and making our quest all the more difficult.

We did spot some Oystercatchers, a Curlew and half a dozen Turnstones – the 150th species I have seen in Somerset. But the Purple Sandpipers were either somewhere else, or hiding.

The sudden switch from frosty to mild weather had brought out swarms of small flying insects, and the birds were having a field day. Robins, Wrens and a smart Grey Wagtail were all taking advantage of the sudden boom in food, with the wagtail leaping elegantly into the air and snapping its bill shut every few seconds.

As we reached the harbour itself, another small passerine flew overhead, uttering a distinctive high-pitched note. I suspected, it turned out correctly, that this was a Rock Pipit. A few seconds later it landed, and Daniel and I were treated to excellent views of this often overlooked little bird.

Larger and bulkier than its commoner relative the Meadow Pipit, it is also a much darker bird: almost grey-green, with a pale throat, plain upperparts and white underparts heavily streaked with dark blotches. The bill is also very distinctive: long and slightly uptilted. Using the telescope, even though the bird was only a few yards away, revealed a surprising beauty to what on first sight looks like just another 'little brown job'.

On the way home, just as it got dark, we had a close – and potentially very unpleasant – encounter with a pair of Roe Deer, which sprang across the road in front of the car. Fortunately the driver following behind us was as alert as I was, and the deer walked off, shocked but safe, flashing their white tails as they disappeared into the darkness.

CHRISTMAS EVE

Mill Batch

Driving off to work the other day I flushed a male Bullfinch from the hedgerow by the side of our garden. Unfortunately, by the time I had worked out its identity from its white rump and flash of cherry-pink, it had disappeared into the foliage.

Then, this morning, as I wandered down the lane, I heard the scolding of Blue Tits from the opposite hedge. Behind them, another bird, skulking amongst the twigs. Surely that red breast was too rich, too pink to be that of a Robin? Yes, it was a male Bullfinch, together with another; and I had brief but good views of these beautiful birds. As they flew off, my ears detected the faintest sound: a gentle, plaintive, almost melancholy 'piu'. Then, as softly as they had come, they were gone.

Bullfinch is a bird I have hoped to see in the garden ever since we arrived, but given both its local and its national scarcity, I thought I might struggle to do so. They are given to wandering in winter, so the spell of colder weather last week may have brought them here.

Like so many birds dependent on hedgerows, they have experienced a steep population decline in recent years. Being fairly shy and retiring, they were never easy to see, even in my youth; but they were always a fairly regular occurrence. Nowadays a year can go by without me coming across a single one, so this duo in my very own backyard was a very welcome sight.

CHRISTMAS DAY

Mill Batch

Two surprises in my 'stocking'. First, a moth trap, bought by Suzanne to encourage my new-found interest in all things lepidopteral. Then, an even bigger surprise: my eldest son David has rigged up a miniature camera inside a nestbox, and linked it up to our television.

Where he gets his technical ability I have no idea (it certainly isn't from me!) but I am truly astounded at his imagination and ingenuity. Two fabulous presents, which I hope will give me plenty to look forward to in the coming year . . .

The Christmas Cup

Today also saw the start of the NHU Christmas Birding Cup – a now established tradition at the BBC Natural History Unit. Started a few years ago by my colleague Martin Hughes-Games, it encourages us to leave the warmth and comfort of our firesides and go birding. The rules are simple:

1. List the number of species you see or hear, in the wild, in Britain, between the start of Christmas Day and the end of New Year's Day (i.e. 00.01 on 25 December to 23.59 on 1 January). Birds in zoos, domestic fowl and pets do not count. Nor does the Christmas turkey.
2. Add them up.
3. Er, that's it.

Earlier this year, Martin left the BBC for the freelance life, so I have taken on responsibility for the competition. To encourage as many people as possible, I have invented several new categories, including one for the number of species seen in, over or from your garden (giving me a sporting chance of at least winning something).

When the competition first began back in the late 1990s, it was a gentlemanly affair, which very few of us took seriously. As a result, it was quite easy to win – in the very first competition I triumphed with about 75 species, easily ahead of the runner-up.

Then things got serious. A couple of years ago, three people (actually two individuals and a couple) broke the century mark, with my friend and colleague Brett Westwood scoring 118. Revenge was promised, but the following year Brett won again, with an incredible 134 species – about as many as you can find in Britain in the winter months.

This year, the committee (well, me actually) decided that Brett would not take part, just to give others a chance. Now, with a full five days to go, I am on about 70 species. With a trip out to East Somerset on Sunday, and a 'Big Day' on 1 January, I might even break the 90 mark. Whether that will be enough to win the whole competition, I am unsure, but at least it should give me a more respectable score than in recent years!

Brean Beach

A family walk is always a good excuse for a spot of impromptu birding, so I took my binoculars along to the beach at Brean. Along with three children, five adults and a dog. And as with most family walks at Christmas, we didn't manage to get out of the house until mid-morning, which meant that we arrived at the beach about three hours after high tide.

Normally I only come birding here at – or soon after – high water, so it was a shock to see just how far out the sea retreats in such a short time. Acres of wet sand had been revealed, and in the milky light all seemed to merge together into a single, grey-brown mass. I was reminded of a line by Philip Larkin, originally written about the flatlands of Lincolnshire, which I shall paraphrase to suit my own location:

Where sky and *Somerset* and water meet.

Looking out over the vastness of the beach, it was hard to imagine there would be any life there at all – apart from the usual dog walkers and their pets. But as I gazed, even with the naked eye, tiny dots began to emerge into view. Using binoculars, I could resolve them into images, and even identify some of them.

Gulls, mostly: a mixture of Black-headed, Herring and Lesser Black-backed. A few Oystercatchers and a small group of Curlews.

And dozens of Shelduck – that strange halfway house between a duck and a goose – wading out into the shallow pools by the distant tideline.

It was only as we were walking back, and the children were getting tired enough to need carrying, that I noticed another group of birds, feeding on the wet sand a hundred yards or so up the beach. At first I took them to be Dunlin, but something about their speed and feeding actions, and their pale plumage, led me to think they might be more interesting.

So George and I strode towards the sea, and sure enough, a closer view revealed them to be a couple of dozen Sanderlings. The rest of the large flock I saw back in late August departed south long ago and are now sunning themselves along the Banc d'Auguin in Mauritania, or some other exotic winter retreat. Why this little party of birds have decided to stay put on Bridgwater Bay is beyond me – perhaps, compared to their breeding grounds in the High Arctic, this place is a tropical paradise.

On the way home, the hedgerows along the route through Lympsham and Tarnock were dotted with Kestrels: perhaps half a dozen in all, each perched on a branch above the road, staring down intently for their prey of field voles.

During the winter, Kestrels tend to hunt by waiting and watching rather than hovering, which, although highly effective, simply uses too much energy during the cold weather. As a result, at this time of year we get a much better view of these beautiful little falcons.

Farther on, the fields along Kingsway, the road between the children's nursery and our home, were filled with Fieldfares and Redwings, together with two hen Pheasants, looking rather lost in this open country. Anyone with a shotgun could have bagged them for a Boxing Day dinner with ease.

Later this afternoon, my future brother-in-law Luke and I took a stroll down the lane behind the house with his dog Gabriella (a rather large and enthusiastic Weimaraner) and George and Daisy.

We had barely reached the end of our garden when a slim, sparrow-like bird with a long tail popped out and dived across the road into the hedge. I suspected it was a Reed Bunting, and sure enough, I saw enough of its white outer tail-feathers, chestnut plumage and dark head to be sure. Not quite *in* the garden, but certainly viewable *from*, so counts as number 71 for the garden list. Roll on 2008, when I shall aim to bring numbers up to a round 80 . . .

Meare Heath

A Blue Tit has popped in and out of the nestbox, but too quickly for me to turn on the TV to see what was going on inside!

On the way back from a family lunch in Wells, my father-in-law and I diverted to Meare Heath for an hour's walk before dusk. Mike walks quite slowly because of an arthritic knee, so we took things easy as we progressed along the path – and as a result I saw far more birds than I would usually!

The ice that covered part of the water last week had melted, and the water levels had risen, so there were no Snipe but plenty of Teal and Shoveler and the usual herons. To the left of the path a Stonechat was perched in his usual bush, and Cetti's Warblers and Water Rails continued to call unseen.

Then I spotted a distant Kingfisher whizzing low across the water like a tiny blue-and-orange arrow. It landed and, although distant, we enjoyed a view of it perched through the telescope. Rather more surprising was a Jay – only the second I have ever seen here in this reedy landscape.

But what we really hoped to see were, of course, the Starlings, and although there were fewer than in previous years, they didn't disappoint. With about half an hour to go before dusk fell, great squadrons of them passed over our heads – thousands, sometimes tens of thousands, in each tight flock.

When they were directly above us, the rapid beating of their wings made a faint whooshing sound, like the wind passing through a stand of trees – almost too faint to hear. Something stirred in my subconscious, and I recalled that the collective noun for Starlings is a 'murmuration' – from the sound that has been described as 'an immense, sibilant rustle'.

Mike and I watched as the birds gathered over the reedbed on the far side of the water, then swept across the reeds and back again like a vast flock of locusts. How they avoid bumping into each other is a mystery, but for the few dozen people in the watching Christmas holiday crowd, the Starlings had delivered on their promise, and we went home happy.

The Egret has landed

Towards the end of the year, a flurry of reports of Cattle Egrets appeared on the SOS website. By late December, there were at least four birds present, scattered around Somerset – which was extraordinary given that until this year there had only ever been four records of Cattle Egrets in the county at all.

Actually, in some ways it was not all that extraordinary. That's because if you ask birders which species they think will be the next to colonise Britain, Cattle Egret would be top of most people's lists.

This is arguably the world's most successful bird. Originally found in Africa, Asia and southern Europe, the Cattle Egret has expanded its range during the past century to reach Australasia, North and South America, and holds the honour of being one of only two species to have been recorded in all seven of the world's continents – including Antarctica. (The other, in case you're wondering, is that great global voyager, the Arctic Tern.)

In the past few decades they have moved northwards through Europe at an astonishing rate, and now breed in good numbers just the other side of the Channel. With more than fifty birds currently at large in the West Country, it surely won't be long before they follow their close relative the Little Egret and start to breed in Britain.

I did finally catch up with a Somerset Cattle Egret – the fifth for the county in about a month. Having risen early to catch the high tide at Steart, I arrived at the field where it had been seen just as the sun rose, and was rewarded with excellent views.

It helped that there was a Little Egret in the same field for comparison. The Cattle Egret looked much more hunched than its elegant relative: noticeably smaller, and with a shorter neck and legs. Closer to, the Cattle Egret's thick yellow bill (the Little Egret's bill is black) also stood out. And as it grubbed around for worms and other invertebrates amongst the feet of about twenty cattle, it looked perfectly at home.

I have no doubt that within the next five or ten years, Cattle Egrets will be virtually as common as Little Egrets are now. I look forward to seeing one fly over Mill Batch some time soon . . .

SUNDAY 30 DECEMBER

East Somerset

Back in July, I spent a morning in the east of the county with local birder John Hansford. But although we had a pleasant walk through his local woods, the weather was against us, and we saw more rain than birds.

So on the penultimate day of the year I went back again; and this time the forecast was more favourable. Our first location was Asda Ponds near Frome, a set of newly landscaped lakes created as compensation for a supermarket development on the outskirts of the town.

We spent a few minutes setting up John's new telescope, adjusting all the usual screws, bolts and angles, until it was finally ready for use. Unfortunately, conditions were too foggy to see much more than a flock of gulls.

After a quick refresher course in gull identification (John does most of his birding in woodland and farmland habitats and until now has tended to ignore them!), we moved onto one of John's home patches, the Orchardleigh estate. A pleasant, though rather muddy, walk produced the first good sighting of the day. Feeding on the ground beneath the trees was a small, active little bird with a greyish-brown body and sleek black crown: a Marsh Tit.

In this month's *Birdwatching* magazine, Graham Appleton of the British Trust for Ornithology has written a timely piece about the recent decline of Marsh Tits. Once fairly common and widespread across southern Britain, they seem to be mirroring the fate of their close relative, the now very scarce Willow Tit. So it was good to hear the rather sneezy 'pitch-oo' call from this particular individual.

In my part of Somerset, arable farmland is almost non-existent, so there are several species I have yet to see in the county. Top of that target list is my favourite bunting, the Yellowhammer. So on our way to our next destination, John took a diversion across a promising looking piece of farmland.

We stopped for a much-needed thermos of coffee on the brow of a hill and almost immediately spotted a little flock of birds in flight. As they posed nicely in the top of a hedgerow, the view through my telescope revealed the characteristic long, slender shape and custard yellow head of a male Yellowhammer, accompanied by several drabber females.

The name 'Yellowhammer' often puzzles novice birders: just what part of the bird is the 'hammer'? In fact, like so many of our ancient bird names, this is a corruption of an Anglo-Saxon term meaning 'small bird' – so Yellowhammer simply means 'little yellow bird'.

John's main local patch is a private wood near the village of Edford. This, he promised, was a 'dead cert' for Treecreepers. As with so many dead certs this proved to be a trifle optimistic. Although we saw plenty of Nuthatches, Marsh Tits and Coal Tits (the latter showing the pale patch on the back of the neck that distinguishes them from Marsh and Willow Tits), we 'dipped out' (to use twitchers' parlance) on the Treecreepers.

Compensation came in the form of one of my very favourite birds. A stream by the entrance to a local farm produced a squat little bird, sitting happily on a small rock in the midst of rushing water: one of the resident Dippers. It hardly moved, apart from the occasional blink, revealing a flash of white across the dark eye – the waterproof membrane that helps this amazing little creature see underwater.

By now time was against us, as I needed to be home in time to take the children to the local park before darkness fell. So we took a swift walk around a farm in the village of Holcombe. I say village, but in fact all that remains of this place is a little church, nestling in a hollow behind the farm buildings.

The history is a fascinating one: after the Black Death killed almost the whole population, in 1348, the houses were demolished and buried to try to prevent the plague spreading. Nothing was ever rebuilt, so the church is the only sign that the village was ever here. According to some sources, the nursery rhyme 'Ring-a-ring o'roses' originated at this very spot.

As we drove past the farm, I was surprised to see a flock of Red-legged Partridges – not just on the track, but perched up on the farm buildings as well – confirming the widely-held belief that the famous 'partridge in a pear tree' is of this rather than our native variety, the Grey Partridge.

The farm itself was a fine example of how to manage land in a wildlife-friendly way. The hedgerows, copses and woods held plenty of birds, including a fine male Bullfinch calling rather more loudly than usual, which momentarily baffled us until we caught sight of its cherry-pink plumage. And a field of crops grown for cattle food contained a small flock of Chaffinches and a few Reed Buntings.

Just before we returned to the car, we heard a brief but unmistakable call – a high-pitched 'pee-pee-pee-pee-pee'. It could only be that most elusive of all woodland birds, a Lesser Spotted Woodpecker, but despite much searching we could not find it again. Apart from this minor disappointment, it had been a great morning's birding in excellent company, and a fine way to finish the year.

Epilogue

Mill Batch

Halfway along our back garden, facing west towards the setting sun, is the bench which used to belong to my mother. For many years it was on the back lawn of her house in Shepperton, my childhood home.

The very last time I saw her, a week or so before she died, we sat together on this same bench on a sunny April afternoon, enjoying the sight of her prized flowerbeds and the sounds of spring birdsong.

So late this afternoon, when I needed some peace and quiet, I did what I often do. I took a wander down the garden and spent a few minutes sitting alone on my mother's bench, soaking up the atmos-phere on this winter's afternoon, the very last of the year.

It's been a rather quiet month in the garden, mainly because of the very mild weather – something I suppose we must get used to. Today is no exception, and apart from the usual birds – Robins singing their plaintive winter song, Blackbirds chattering nosily in the bushes, and the chorus of cawing Rooks – there's nothing unusual going on.

Then, as dusk begins to fall, I hear a familiar series of high-pitched, rather sneeze-like calls from the row of pollarded willows behind me. It's a little party of Long-tailed Tits, making their way along the trees in search of tiny insects, and calling constantly to one another as they go.

The final surprise of the year in the garden, and a wonderfully inti-mate one, as these tiny birds hang from the twigs of the willow trees, pause briefly to feed, and then move on, their chirpy little calls fading away into the gloom.

I reflect on the birds I have seen this year – many of them from the very spot where I am sitting now. The first Chiffchaff, chirping away in the same willows on a blustery day in March; the lone Whimbrel flying northwards on a sunny May Day evening; or the Raven croak-ing in next door's orchard one morning in October.

It has been a very enjoyable year, probably because I've done the vast majority of my birding within a few miles of home. I have learned – or maybe relearned – a simple but important lesson. That watching birds where I live – in my garden, local patch and the county of Somerset – is just as rewarding as dashing around the coun-try trying to see rarities or visiting exotic foreign locations.

I have also realised that some of my most memorable encounters with birds were when I came across a familiar species in an un-familiar place or at an unexpected time: like those roosting Pied

Wagtails we saw after a family outing to the pictures back in October. That's what I love about birding: it's what you might call the Martini pastime – one you can do 'any time, any place, anywhere . . .'

The people with whom I have watched birds during the course of this year are equally important. For me birding can never be an entirely solitary pastime; although I do love being out on my own, my most treasured memories of this year are those I shared with my family and friends – some birders, others not. I owe them all a great debt.

In the end I tallied a modest but respectable 81 in the Christmas Cup, coming fourth out of a dozen or so participants. Brett, without even really trying, scored 90, while the winner was our research librarian Rob, who didn't quite manage to break the 100 barrier with 98. I consoled myself with the fact that he travelled to several well-known birding sites during the holidays, whereas I took a more gentlemanly approach, staying entirely in my local area. But the point of the competition is to encourage colleagues to take up birding – some of them for the very first time. The enthusiasm with which they took part – and the delightful accounts of sightings of Snow Buntings in Norfolk, Eider Ducks in Northumberland or just the ducks in a local park – are what real birding is all about.

The highlight of the year? Out of so many, it is almost impossible to pick out a single one. But the simple pleasure of sitting in the back garden and listening to birdsong on a fine spring day, while the children blow dandelion clocks, pick buttercups and chase butterflies, is pretty hard to beat.

This is my own little piece of England, and although I have been here for less than two years, it seems much longer. And the thought that Suzanne and I intend to stay here for the rest of our lives, and watch Charlie, George and Daisy grow up to love this place and its birds as much as we do, is a good one on which to end the old year and welcome the new.

Now, as darkness falls, and a final squadron of Starlings shoots over-head on their way to roost, there's just time to put on my Buzz Lightyear costume before our friends arrive for supper . . .

Acknowledgements

M any people went birding, corresponded with or discussed birds with me during the course of this year, and I should like to thank them all for their companionship and enthusiasm.

In alphabetical order, they are: Chris Baines, Kevin Bayes, Nigel, Clare, Rachel and Thomas Bean, Simon Beard, Catherine Biggs, Sarah Blunt, Marek Borkowski, Jolie Bradfield, Jeremy Bristow and family, John Burrell, Sue Caola, George Chamier, John Clare, Rob Collis, Graham Coster, Dominic Couzens, Phil and Frances Craig, Luke Davie, Andrew Dawes, Mike Dilger, June and Mike Dolan, Shelley Dolan, Alison Everett, Brian Gibbs, John Hansford, John Hawkins, Josep del Hoyo, Ian Hull, Simon Humphries, Simon King, Lasse Laine, Matthew and Oscar Lee, Sheila Lego, Rod Leslie, Mick Lockyer, Nick Martin, Neil McKillop, Cathy Mordaunt, Marleen Murgitroyde, Jeremy Mynott, Simon Nash, Ken Neil, Daniel Osorio, David and Martine Osorio, Steve Phillipps, Rick Popham, Nigel and Cheryle

Redman, Jimmy and Rosie Reid, Chris Rose, Ian Salvage, Mark Sheen, Nick Smith-Baker, Ken Spencer, Miranda and Jemma Sturgess and family, Richard, Sonja and Finn Taylor-Jones, Alan Titchmarsh, Graham Turner, Keith Vinicombe, Katie Walker, Simon Ware, Chris Watson, Brett Westwood, Mac and Hilary Wright and Martin and Barbara Woodcock.

Once again, my thanks to everyone involved in producing this book, including copy-editor Dan Steward. The beautiful cover was created by that fine artist Robert Gillmor, while Carry Akroyd provided the relief prints for the chapter openers.

My greatest thanks go to my friend and publisher Graham Coster, for coming up with the idea for the book and for steering it through to a successful conclusion with his usual tact and expertise. I also acknowledge the *Guardian*, in whose pages some of this material appeared in various forms.

Finally, of course, to my wonderful family: my wife Suzanne and my children David, James, Charlie, George and Daisy – some of whom, at least, share my passion for birds!

Stephen Moss
Mark, Somerset; March 2008